# THE SCHOOL
# EDUCATION OF
# GIRLS

# THE SCHOOL EDUCATION OF GIRLS

An international
comparative study on school wastage
among girls and boys
at the first and second levels
of education

Isabelle Deblé

*Published in 1980 by the United Nations Educational,*
*Scientific and Cultural Organization*
*7 place de Fontenoy, 75700 Paris*
*Printed by Imprimeries Réunies de Chambéry*

*ISBN 92-3-101782-9*
*French edition:   92-3-201728-2*
*Spanish edition: 92-3-301782-6*
*Russian edition: 92-3-401782-X*
*Arabic edition:   92-3-601782-7*

# PREFACE

*In 1967, as a contribution to efforts to improve the status of women, Unesco embarked on a long-term programme to promote equality of educational opportunity between the sexes. This programme is being implemented in a series of planned stages with a view to gaining more insight into the various impediments in the way of schooling for girls and their access to certain types of education and training. The information obtained has been used to devise and test suitable programmes for the prevention or reduction of various forms of discrimination encountered by girls and women in the field of education. Among other themes, these stages were to include studies on co-education, on the access of girls to primary, secondary, technical and higher education, on the access of women to literacy courses and the teaching profession, on the relationship between educational and employment opportunities for women, on equal access for girls and women to education in the context of rural development and on the role of working mothers in the education of their pre-school age children, together with experimental projects aimed at promoting equality of educational opportunity for women and girls and the organization of a number of meetings of experts and seminars. The results of all these activities have been widely circulated.*

*The idea of equal educational opportunity for all has come a long way. No country now challenges its basic premise and national officials are endeavouring to give it substance by mobilizing available resources. As a result, the enrolment ratios for girls in primary education has risen considerably in almost all countries, though in many cases it is still lower than that for boys. The first essential step is to enrol an increasing number of girls in schools, so as to arrive at equal numbers for the two sexes; but numerical balance is just one of the aspects of equal educational opportunity. It is also essential to take other measures and ensure, for example, that girls study for the same length of time as boys and reach the same levels of instruction. In 1977-78 Unesco set in motion a major programme, in its desire to learn more about the causes of wastage in the education of girls, to identify measures and programmes designed to solve this problem and to work out proposals for supporting action in this field. This programme has three aspects: an inter-*

national study based on a questionnaire sent to all Member States, a series of country studies entrusted to national teams in Australia, Benin, Burma, Mexico and the Syrian Arab Republic, and a programme to foster the exchange of information and experimental data whose budget included provision for study missions. In this connection, it should be mentioned that the World Conference of International Women's Year (Mexico, 1975) drew attention to the fact that educational wastage among girls was a major barrier to the advancement of women. This is also one of the problems concerning which the countries taking part in the World Plan of Action for the Implementation of the Objectives of the International Women's Year have been asked to take suitable measures in the course of the United Nations Decade for Women (1976-85).

The present study, a Unesco contribution to this Decade, was carried out by Miss Isabelle Deblé of the Institut d'Étude du Développement Économique et Social at the University of Paris I, by means of her own research activities, information kindly supplied by sixty-two Member States[1] in response to the questionnaire (Appendix I) and data at the disposal of the Unesco Office of Statistics.

The author of this study, to whom the Secretariat would like to express its gratitude, is responsible for the selection and presentation of the facts analysed and for the opinions expressed, which are not necessarily those of Unesco and do not in any way commit the Organization. The designations employed by the author and her presentation of the material do not imply the expression of any opinion whatsoever on the part of Unesco concerning the legal status of any country or territory, town or zone or its authorities, or concerning the delimitations of the frontiers of any country or territory. However, an effort has been made to employ as far as possible the official designations of countries in force at the time this study was completed.

---

1. Argentina, Australia, Austria, Bahrain, Barbados, Belgium, Benin, Bolivia, Bulgaria, Byelorussian Soviet Socialist Republic, Central African Empire, Chad, Chile, Costa Rica, Cyprus, Czechoslovakia, Denmark, Dominican Republic, Finland, France, Gabon, German Democratic Republic, Germany (Federal Republic of), Ghana, Greece, Guatemala, Iran, Iraq, Israel, Ivory Coast, Japan, Jordan, Kuwait, Lebanon, Malta, Mauritania, Mexico, Morocco, Nepal, Netherlands, New Zealand, Norway, Pakistan, Peru, Philippines, Poland, Portugal, Qatar, Spain, Sri Lanka, Sudan, Sweden, Syrian Arab Republic, Tunisia, Union of Soviet Socialist Republics, United Republic of Cameroon, United Republic of Tanzania, United States of America, Uruguay, Venezuela, Yemen, Zambia.

# CONTENTS

## PART THREE

### THE CAUSES OF FEMALE WASTAGE

## PART FOUR

### THE STRUGGLE AGAINST FEMALE WASTAGE IN EDUCATION

Chapter Two.    *Measures specially aimed at reducing female*
                                *wastage in education*                           122

Chapter Three.    *The measures adopted: scope and future outlook*    125


APPENDIXES

# INTRODUCTION

The term 'wastage'[1] covers phenomena of particular interest to educators, sociologists and economists. Many teachers are troubled by the fact that a large number of pupils do not progress at the normal rate set by the educational authorities. When no more than a minority of children manage to satisfy the system's standard requirements, the school itself is called into question, especially when its declared objective is to provide an identical course of instruction for all pupils. The sociologist seeks to clarify the links between the school as an institution and society, in the hope that they will account for some of the unsatisfactory conditions of schooling experienced by many groups of children. Economic analysis, on the other hand, asks whether the system of education is quantitatively and qualitatively as productive as it should be, given its resources.

In 1970, the International Conference of Education, convened in Geneva by Unesco and devoted to 'the improved effectiveness of educational systems particularly through reduction of wastage at all levels of instruction', made it possible to take stock of ongoing research in this field in various parts of the world and especially of two surveys, one conducted by the Unesco Office of Statistics and the other by the International Bureau of Education (IBE). In the next two years two important works were published on the same subject.[2]

However, the conditions under which girls obtain primary or secondary education are still somewhat obscure and the World

---

1. Wastage is 'a combination of two factors—the premature dropping out of pupils before completing a course (say of four years or six years of primary school), and the repetition of grades'— Unesco, *Manual of Educational Statistics*, p. 83–4, Paris, 1961.
2. Unesco, *Wastage in Education; A World Problem*, a study prepared for the International Bureau of Education by M. A. Brimer and L. Pauli, Paris/Geneva, Unesco: IBE, 1971 (Studies and Surveys in Comparative Education); Unesco, *A Statistical Study of Wastage at School*, a study prepared for the International Bureau of Education by the Unesco Office of Statistics, Paris/Geneva, Unesco: IBE, 1972 (Studies and Surveys in Comparative Education).

Conference of International Women's Year (Mexico, 1975) felt that studies should be undertaken to improve our understanding of female wastage. This is the objective of our study, which concentrates on three particular questions: Are the same number of girls and boys admitted to school? Does their schooling follow the same pattern? Are these two aspects related?

It is not our intention to examine schooling in general but only the factors which differentiate girls and boys in a given context. For the forms and general causes of wastage we shall refer to the two works mentioned above but concentrate on aspects of the problem that specifically concern girls.

We make no claim to present a full account of wastage in the education of girls throughout the world, but we shall try to provide as much information as possible on the nature and extent of the problem and on the various forms it takes.

Parts One and Two, therefore, which attempt to identify and measure certain aspects of girls' schooling, are necessarily based on figures and statistical analysis.

Part Three will deal with the causes suggested and perceived by different states and bodies and draw attention to a few hypotheses concerning less explicit causes that emerge from the processing and analysis of available data.

Part Four will describe the steps taken by various countries with a view to providing a range of measures designed to reduce wastage in the education of girls to the greatest possible extent, yet bearing in mind that each state has its own system of education, with its own pattern of organization and above all its own content, and that each system operates within a particular economic, social and cultural context.

PART ONE

# ACCESS OF GIRLS
# TO THE FIRST AND SECOND
# LEVELS OF EDUCATION

## (TOGETHER WITH SOME DATA
## ON POST-SECONDARY EDUCATION)

*A world approach to the problem of girls' schooling raises a great many difficulties. Every state obviously has a decisive say in the organization of its education system, the definition of goals and the various administrative and pedagogical procedures employed. But it is equally self-evident that every system of education is peculiar to a particular society, which in turn embraces a range of more or less heterogeneous classes and socio-cultural groups. In contributing to the development of curricula and teaching methods, modern theories of education and psychology start out from a certain view of childhood that does not usually distinguish between boys and girls and, for nearly a century now, opinion has been urging the school to take in and educate all children in the same way, disregarding sexual differences. But, however we choose to interpret the evolution of human societies, we are obliged to acknowledge the strong sociological differentiation between men and women and between adults and children. Childhood, like adolescence, is increasingly recognized as a distinct period of life, although its length varies with the society. Lastly, the childhood and adolescence of girls and boys are still intimately linked to the male and female attitudes of each cultural group.*

*One of the most significant twentieth-century developments has been the gradual institutionalization of education for children and adolescents, changing attitudes towards schooling on the part of the various social groups and the way in which these groups have responded to what is presented as one of the essential factors of economic and social development. All Unesco Member States have made great efforts to collect an ever-increasing mass of data that satisfy the criteria adopted in common by members of the organization. The Office of Statistics of the Secretariat and the International Institute for Educational Planning are also supporting the attempts of many research centres and ministerial departments to devise indicators that express certain aspects of the evolution of schooling and its manner of operation. But, owing to the variety of structures and content, it is still difficult to compare education systems; and it is even more difficult to obtain comparable data, since methods of collecting information and drawing up statistics vary over*

15

a period of time and from one country to another. Hence the importance of efforts to standardize and the need for cautious handling of the indicators employed to establish a hierarchy of the situations in different states. We shall, however, be obliged to make use of all available indicators, while recognizing that the requirements of number may run counter to the quality of content and that these indicators reflect only part of a given reality. There have been too few in-depth studies on the education of girls as a social phenomenon showing the changing role of women to avoid recourse to a multiplicity of indicators which, though sometimes at odds with one another, may point to issues for further investigation.

Lastly, it should be noted that since the questionnaire did not elicit data suitable for quantitative treatment, the following analyses are based on information published or supplied by the Unesco Office of Statistics.

# CHAPTER ONE

# A STATISTICAL APPROACH

A thorough statistical study of the access of boys and girls to primary and secondary education would require data on population distribution by sex for each group from the age of 5 or 6 to 18 or 19 in a given year and for the same year, the breakdown of pupils at school by sex, age and year of study. It would then be possible to work out comparative ratios of school attendance by age and the level of instruction attained by particular year-groups.

For example: in the year $t$, 80 out of 100 boys aged 7 are at school, with 30 in the first year of primary education, 40 in the second year and 10 in the third; out of 100 girls of the same age, 60 are at school, with 18 in the first year, 35 in the second year and 7 in the third. This imaginary example produces enrolment ratios of 80% and 60% respectively at 7 years of age but, within the school population, a higher proportion of girls are studying in the more advanced courses:

|  | Boys (%) | Girls (%) |
|---|---|---|
| First year | 37.5 | 30.0 |
| Second year | 50.0 | 58.3 |
| Third year | 12.5 | 11.6 |

It might be concluded that, at 7 years old, girls tend to progress more quickly than boys but we do not in fact know whether the girls in question began their formal education earlier than the boys.

The information at our disposal is not full enough for us to undertake a similar study at the world level. Our attempt to pinpoint differences in the access of girls and boys to education is therefore based on a series of indicators already established by

17

Unesco, either by country or for twenty-four regions of the world (as defined by the United Nations Population Division; see Appendix II). Each indicator highlights a particular aspect of comparative schooling for male and female children and adolescents and helps clarify the present educational situation in regard to girls.

COMPARISON OF ENROLMENT RATIOS
FOR GIRLS AND BOYS, BY AGE

For information on sources and on the methods employed for calculation or estimation, the reader is referred to *The Dimensions of School Enrolment*.[1] Table 1[2] which concerns 39 countries—12 in Africa, 6 in Asia, 1 in North America, 4 in Central America, 3 in South America, 12 in Europe and 1 in Oceania—presents figures for only eight year-groups (6, 8, 10, 12, 15, 16, 18, 20 years). These ages were chosen because they bring out *how* and *when* the school attendance of girls in relation to that of boys changes, at important moments during adolescence and early adulthood which correspond to points of transition from one level of education to another. Differences in ratios equal to or above five points are shown by italic figures in the table. The sample is neither statistically representative nor recent, but it provides a fairly accurate picture of the various situations to be found in the world at certain periods.

Of the thirty-nine countries, five (Argentina, Bulgaria, Costa Rica, Cuba and Panama) display ratios that differ by five points or less.

At the ages considered, the enrolment ratios for girls are often higher than those for boys in Argentina, Bulgaria, France, Hungary and Sweden.

On the other hand, boys predominate from the beginning of schooling in 16 of the 39 countries; at 8 years old in 14 (9 African, 2 Latin American and 3 Asian countries) and at 10 years old in 2 countries (Malaysia and Mauritius). These are followed by 4 countries (including 2 from Southern Europe) where differences emerge at 12 years old, and 7 countries (mostly European) where discrimination appears at the age of 15, that is, at the time of adolescence.

In Botswana and New Zealand, female enrolments do not fall behind male enrolments until the age of 16, and until 18 in the

1. Unesco Office of Statistics, *The Dimensions of School Enrolment. A Study of Enrolment Ratios in the World*, Paris, 1975 (Current Studies and Research in Statistics, CSR-E-16).
2. Tables referred to in Part One will be found on pages 32-41.

Federal Republic of Germany, Japan, the United Kingdom and Sweden.

In short, there are more boys at school than girls, but the age at which the difference becomes clear bears no relation to the level or length of education. An examination of Table 1 reveals various types of situation:

1. There may exist a pronounced difference between the sexes from the very beginning of school, whether the country's general level of enrolment is low (Upper Volta in 1967) or quite high (India in 1967).
2. In countries with very high enrolment, the difference appears at a late stage and may be slight (Sweden, 1969) or quite significant (Japan, 1970).
3. The ratios diverge at 8 years old in most developing countries and at 15 in industrialized countries.

COMPARATIVE VALUES FOR GIRLS AND BOYS
OF THE RATIO BETWEEN SCHOOL ENROLMENTS
AND TOTAL POPULATION

In this case we utilize an indicator that measures the intensity of enrolment by relating the total numbers of boys and of girls in each of the three levels of education to the population, aged 6-29.

Table 2 sets forth the results for thirty-nine countries in the most recent year for which information is available. It would seem plausible that the higher a country's intensity of enrolment the less difference there would be between the sexes. However, analysis of the data reveals that this not so and that the discrimination in enrolment between girls and boys is therefore due to causes outside education.

Since the base years mentioned in Table 2 vary considerably it was not considered worth while to arrange the situations in hierarchical order.

The table shows that the differences between the values, calculated separately for each sex, range from—22.3 for Togo to + 6.7 for Kuwait. Five countries display a higher enrolment ratio for girls than for boys. In the other thirty-four countries the situation is the other way round, with significant differences in twenty-two of them.

## COMPARISON OF ENROLMENT RATIOS
### BY AGE-GROUP AND BY SEX

The information here is relatively recent (1975). It covers most of the world and indicates, once again, the extent of education provided and differences between male and female enrolment at various stages of schooling.

Table 3 shows that there exist wide gaps between the enrolment of girls and boys from 6 to 11 years of age, in each case to the detriment of girls in seven of the regions (Eastern Africa, Middle Africa, Northern Africa, Western Africa, Middle South Asia, Western South Asia and Melanesia). In this final quarter of the twentieth century inequality takes root at a very early age and condemns a large proportion of the female population to illiteracy. In these regions it is particularly noteworthy between the ages of 1a and 17 years, where the ratios often vary from single to double. In half the regions of the world half the population thus suffers one of the most potentially damaging types of discrimination for future generations. It is hardly surprising that enrolment ratios differ even more markedly for the 18–23 year age-group; indeed, the proportion of female students in this age-group exceeds 20% in only six regions (Temperate South America, Tropical South America, Northern America, Southern Europe, Western Europe and the USSR).

It should also be noted that this table, which is based on averages, tends to play down the actual situation which, when examined country by country, reveals even greater differences in enrolment by sex.

### COMPARISON OF GROSS ENROLMENT RATIOS
#### BY SEX AND LEVEL OF EDUCATION

Comparison between the school population at a given level of education and the theoretical school-age population at this level produces gross enrolment ratios that cannot be compared from one region to another owing to differences between the systems of education. However, these ratios provide information on the present level of enrolment whereas the preceding ratios covered only school attendance and the system's intake capacity at a particular level. Ratios exceeding 100% indicate, in primary education for instance, that there are more children enrolled in the schools than are contained in the corresponding age-group (6–11 years) because of early or late entry and a more or less considerable number of repeaters.

Table 4 illustrates two phenomena: first, the sudden drop in enrolment between the different levels of education—very sharp in most of the regions considered, the only exceptions being Northern America, Japan, Northern, Southern and Western Europe and, to a lesser extent, Australia and New Zealand; and, second, the way in which this drop is differentiated according to sex. Since the same bases were employed for calculation it is possible to compare the resulting figures for boys and girls: in regions already noted for wide variations by age-group, the gaps broaden and show how, between levels of education, female enrolments fall more quickly than male enrolments. There thus appear to exist differences both in access to education and in the actual school career, whose negative consequences are cumulative.

In the developed regions the ratios are close to or distinctly more than 100 per cent at the first level. It is at the second level that they are at their highest in comparison to the world average (70.4% and 71.5% for boys and girls respectively, as against 45.81% and 40.55%). It will be noted that the ratios vary very little by sex at each of those two levels and that the ratios for girls are often higher than those for boys. Generally speaking, the degree of enrolment does not drop sharply between levels, except in Temperate South America, Eastern Europe and the USSR.

For the developing regions, it seemed useful to distinguish those in which the first-level enrolment ratios, for boys at least, are under 100% from the ones in which it is 100% or more.

When the ratio is under 100% (Eastern, Northern and Western Africa, Eastern South Asia, Middle South Asia, Western South Asia and Melanesia), boys always outnumber girls at a given level, though the difference is less marked in the countries of Eastern South Asia. In these regions primary education is less developed and transition from one level to the next implies that more girls will be eliminated than boys.

In regions with ratios of 100% or over (Middle Africa, Southern Africa, Caribbean, Middle America, Tropical South America, other East Asia, Polynesia and Micronesia, that is, in countries with a larger intake capacity, the difference between the ratios for each sex is small (except in Middle Africa).

On the other hand, the differences from one level to the next show that selection procedures are always much more severe for girls and that boys receive considerable preferential treatment for admission to secondary education.

These remarks apply even more to the third level. In little

21

developed regions, the ratios are always higher for boys than for girls, ranging from 0.7% to 10.5% for male students and from 0.2% to 7.5% for female students; moreover, when the division into two groups of regions based on the extension of first-level education is applied, the gap between the highest and lowest ratios once again turns out to be more pronounced for girls than for boys. The lower the level of development of primary education, the more serious are the obstacles that girls have to overcome in order to accede to higher education.

Even though enrolment falls sharply between the second and third levels, the situation in developed countries is much better, but the ratios by sex, often well balanced or even to the advantage of girls at the lower levels, are always higher for boys, except in Eastern Europe and the USSR.

These general comments sketch the broad outline of the comparative 1975 situation of boys and girls in the three levels of education, but they clearly do not go far enough to pinpoint the moments in the course of education when discrimination exerts a decisive influence.

### DISPARITIES IN SCHOOL ATTENDANCE ACCORDING TO SOCIO-GEOGRAPHICAL MILIEU AND OCCUPATIONAL BACKGROUND

The analysis of female wastage cannot stop at inter-country comparisons: we must also take the variety of situations within a given country into consideration. It is now general knowledge that geographical variables have a decisive impact on enrolment: the chances of going to school depend on the region in which a person lives, and this usually strengthens the inequalities between boys and girls.

To illustrate this point where primary education is concerned with an example from Tunisia, the proportion (percentage) of girls in primary education in certain governorates in 1975 was as follows: Le Kef, 37.3; Tendouba, 34; South Tunis, 36; Nabeul, 43; Bedja, 35; Kasserine, 30.6; Siliana, 34; Bizerte, 42; Sousse, 41; Monastir, 42; Mahdia, 29.6[1].

The variations by governorate are considerable but become even more striking as population density decreases: in sparsely populated

---

1. Saïda Mahfoudh, 'Scolarisation et emploi féminins', *Revue Tunisienne des sciences de l'éducation* (Tunis), No. 6, 1977, p. 89–126.

areas girls account for between 16.6% and 36% of pupils but in towns of over 50,000 inhabitants the proportion reaches 45–49%.

It is agreed that urbanization tends to reduce inequalities in access to education, but there are not enough detailed studies to provide a clear picture of actual situations and their true causes.

We have also learned to appreciate the importance of family influence. Table 5 shows that even in France, which is adequately provided with secondary schools, the enrolment ratio for girls correlates with the family's occupational category.

CHAPTER TWO

# RECENT DEVELOPMENTS
# AND FUTURE PROSPECTS

Since 1950 a growing number of publications on education have stressed the enormous increase in pupil numbers in all countries and at all levels of education.[2] The twentieth century—and especially its second half— has in fact witnessed the most vigorous efforts to institutionalize and generalize education that the world has ever seen.

A Unesco situation report for the period 1960–69, quoted in the remarkable book *Learning to Be*[3] produced by the International Commission on the Development of Education, described the characteristic features of this growth in enrolments and stressed the impact of population increases, particularly in regions with the lowest enrolment ratios to begin with. The greatest increases in pupil numbers were to be found in the three continents containing the largest number of developing states.

It should be recalled that the rapid expansion of pupil numbers throughout the world during the first half of the 1960s later slowed down in every major region, although it remained high in Africa and the Arab states.

The growth in female pupil numbers, again at the world level, was equal to that of total enrolments except in the case of higher education where it was more rapid, indicating that the proportion of girls did not change between 1960 and 1969. Yet in 1960, the situation was far from ensuring equal participation in education for both sexes; in consequence we are obliged to conclude that, even though ideas and customs have evolved, there is as yet no evidence of a decisive step towards the elimination of flagrant inequality between girls and boys.

1. Most of these considerations are drawn from a comparative study being prepared by the Unesco Office of Statistics on the enrolment of boys and girls.
2. Generally speaking, these studies are based on statistics that do not include the People's Republic of China, the Democratic People's Republic of Korea and the Socialist Republic of Viet Nam.
3. E. Faure et al., *Learning to Be*, Paris/London, Unesco/Harrap, 1972.

24

*Learning to Be* points out that

differences are marked in education for girls and women. In North America, Europe and Latin America, school enrolments of boys and girls at primary and secondary levels are approximately equal. But grouping Africa, Asia and the Arab States together, we find 50 per cent more boys than girls in primary schools, and 100 per cent more in secondary schools. World illiteracy figures show further the extent to which women are at a disadvantage; some 40 per cent are estimated to be illiterate, compared with 28 per cent of men.[1]

Today, an examination of the evolution of the proportion of girls at school in the 6–11, 12–17 and 18–23 age-groups during the period 1965–70 and in 1975 gives rise to the following observations:

First, in regard to the group aged 6–11 years, the percentage of girls has risen in eight regions,[2] dropped slightly in Temperate South America and remained stable in fourteen other regions. The increases have taken place in developing countries with the most unfavourable situation to begin with and have generally been minimal with the greatest improvement in Middle Africa (5%).

Second, for the group aged 12–17 years, the proportion of girls has risen more often, for such a trend may be observed in fifteen of the regions considered; but, as a rule, the increase is most significant in the same regions as before, that is, in regions with relatively little educational provision, and the proportion of girl pupils is still low (32% in Middle South Asia, 33% in Melanesia, 37% in Africa as a whole). In the other regions it has progressed slowly, by one or two points, to reach 49% in the most favourable cases. It should be noted that, in 1975, this figure had not yet been attained in Middle America (43%), Eastern South Asia (44%) or Southern Europe (46%). In the USSR and Temperate South America (especially Argentina) there are more girls of this age-group at school than boys (51%).

Finally, as regards the group aged 18–23 years, there has been a more marked change between 1965 and 1975, especially in the regions with already extensive educational provision at this level. The proportion of girls increased by five to ten points in all the regions of Europe, in the USSR and in East Asia. There was a sharp increase in Northern Africa (+9%), although the proportion is still low (30%), and in Tropical South America (+6%). However, enrolment ratios for girls aged between 18 and 23 years never reach 50% except in Eastern Europe and the USSR.

---

1. Faure et al., op. cit., p. 52.
2. Eastern Africa, Middle Africa, Northern Africa, Western Africa, Carribbean, East Asian countries except Japan, Middle South Asia and Western South Asia.

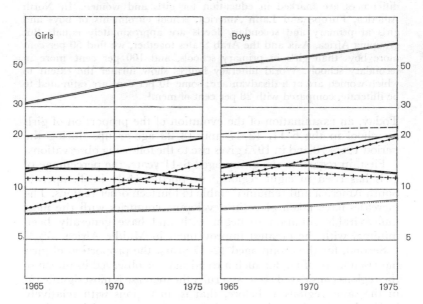

6–11 age-group

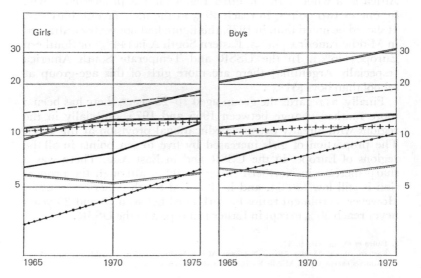

12–17 age-group

26

18–23 age-group

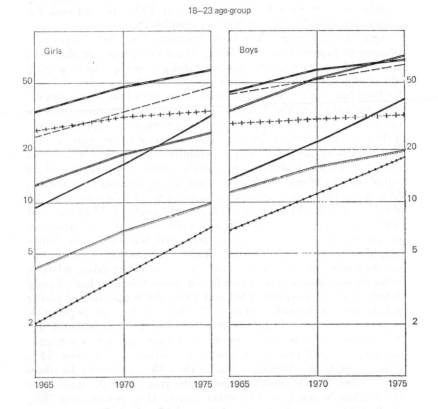

FIG. 1.   Evolution of enrolments by age-group (in millions).

*Source*; Unesco Office of Statistics, *Étude comparative de la scolarisation des filles et des garçons; une analyse statistique 1965-1975* (to be published in the series 'Enquêtes et recherches: travaux en cours').

The graphs in Figure 1 display these facts and show that if trends remain as they were between 1965 and 1975, the outlook for future education of girls at school is rather bleak.

Apart from Europe, Northern America, East Asia (especially because of Japan) and the USSR, where enrolments in the 6–11 and 12–18 age-groups have either stabilized or slightly increased, the school population has risen sharply at all educational levels for both boys and girls, but in many cases 1975 female enrolments have only reached the 1965 level for boys. The ongoing study of the Unesco Office of Statistics appears to conclude that girls have little hope of catching up with the male enrolment ratios. This particularly applies to developing countries which have to contend with two major problems: a quickly rising population and an initial pattern of schooling very much to the disadvantage of girls. Moreover, the percentages sometimes conceal differences in the absolute numbers of boys and girls attending school. Most national studies reveal improved enrolment ratios for girls and a higher proportion of girls among those admitted but disregard demographic data on boys and girls. This oversight can have serious consequences. In this connection, it is worth recalling what a study on out-of-school youth in fifteen Asian countries had already noted in 1974: between 1960 and 1970, the proportion of young people not at school[1] fell to 53% but, owing to population increases, their actual number rose by 19 million, to 182 million.[2] This phenomenon is even more serious where girls are concerned: in 1960, 71% of girls were not in education (as against 54% of boys) and, in 1970, 62% (as against 45% of boys). In absolute figures, female out-of-school youth rose from 91 million to 104 million in ten years; in other words, they represented 56% of all children not at school in 1960 and 57% in 1970.

The number of non-enrolled boys and girls 6–12 years old has been tending to fall, both in percentage and in absolute terms (although only slightly in the latter case), but in every case the figures show a bigger drop for boys than for girls (in 1960, 59% of out-of-school youth were girls; in 1970, 62%).

When we turn to the 12–17 age-group, we note that, between 1960 and 1970, the ratio of non-enrolment fell from 80% to 76% but that actual numbers rose by 24 million (from 85 to 109 million). As usual, girls are more seriously affected than boys: the

---

1. Including those who have never been to school, those who are admitted but then drop out before completing primary education and those who complete primary education but then drop out or suspend their studies.
2. Unesco Office of Statistics, *The Statistical Dimension of Out-of-School Youth in Asia*, Paris, 1974 (Current Studies and Research in Statistics, CSR-E-6).

ratio of non-enrolled girls fell from 87% to 83% only and, in 1970, they accounted for 54.1% of out-of-school youth, as against 52.9% in 1960.

Studies of this type should be carried out for all regions of the world to enable the various trends to be more closely followed and compared.

When we come to analyse the evolution of enrolments by level of instruction rather than by age-group, we end up with similar results even though differences in the education systems (length of each level, age at admission, etc.) makes inter-regional comparison a delicate matter.

In South Asia, for example, the number of girls in the first and second levels of education had, by 1975, barely reached the 1965 figure for boys; Africa presents a similar picture at the first level but the second-level situation has slightly improved. Table 6 shows the proportion of female pupils in 1965, 1970 and 1975 for all three levels of instruction. It should be noted that there exists no relation between the intensity of enrolment and the percentage of girls and that numerical equality may be found in a country with little educational provision and low female participation in one with a relatively high enrolment ratio. The table shows that things have not greatly changed for girls in relation to boys and that the regions may be classed in much the same order in 1975 as they were in 1965. The largest increases in female enrolments are to be found in the regions whose education was the least developed to begin with, and this holds for all levels with, however, the biggest gains at the second level. In the course of ten years the lowest and highest figures for the proportion of girls at school in the seven most disadvantaged regions[1] rose at the first level, from 34% and 40% in 1965, to 36% and 40% in 1970, and to 38% and 42% in 1975; at the second level, from 22% and 31% in 1965, to 26% and 33% in 1970, and to 29% and 35% in 1975. In the other sixteen regions of the world the variations are slight at the first level but much more apparent later.

In regions with a high birth rate, and despite the fact that the general population growth rate is higher for girls, more boys start school each year than girls. In absolute terms, the gap between the number of boys and girls at school is widening. Basing their analysis mainly on pupil numbers in the first year of primary education, statisticians point out that the gaps between enrolment ratios are closing slightly, at least in primary education, but abso-

---

1. Eastern Africa, Middle Africa, Northern Africa, Western Africa, Middle South Asia, Western South Asia and Melanesia.

lute differences are increasing in all age-groups and in all levels of instruction.

Appendixes III, IV, V, and VI show that, in a group of nearly 100 developing countries, enrolment ratios for the 6–23 age-group ranged, between 1965 and 1975, from under 10% to over 70% (taking boys and girls separately). Table 7 gives the number of countries by enrolment ratio for this age-group.

Even though ratios have improved for both sexes, girls have still not caught up. The projection of trends observed in the period between 1965 and 1975 gives rise to the following forecasts.

For the 6–11 age-group, differences between enrolment ratios will continue to narrow yet remain very significant, especially in Africa and South Asia. For the 12–17 age-group, the gap will widen in Africa, Latin America and Southern Europe and narrow slightly in Asia, though it will still be very wide in South Asia (15.1). For the 18–23 age-group the gap will widen everywhere except in Europe, Northern America and the USSR.

In absolute figures, the gap will narrow in Latin America for the 6–11 age-group, in East Asia for the 6–11 and 12–17 age-groups, in Europe for the 6-11 age-group, and in the USSR for primary education but with an increasing gap in favour of girls in the 12–17 age-group.

Elsewhere the gap will increasingly favour boys and become very wide in Middle South Asia. In 1985, if present trends continue, the world as a whole will contain 37 million more boys at school than girls in the 6–11 age-group, with 34,780,000 of them in developing countries. It may thus be said that the prospects for equal opportunity for boys and girls are distant, even in primary education.

CONCLUSIONS

There can be no doubt that without a fundamental and resolute will to bring about change, finding expression in carefully studied and co-ordinated practical measures, equal access to education for girls and boys might well prove unattainable in several parts of the world. This reflection gives special significance to the study of wastage among female pupils. We have in fact spent quite a long time on the first part of our study precisely because it exerts a considerable influence on the second. Comparing the school career of two groups of pupils which are quantitively so unevenly balanced is tantamount to stacking the cards from the start. It is clear that the limited recruitment of girls operates in each country through mechanisms which necessarily end up by setting them apart from boys in a great variety of ways. It is well known, for example, that female participation in education is higher in towns than in rural areas and that parents who send their daughters to school against the prevailing custom are in a minority and hence tend to stand out. From the first day of school, individual girls have by no means the same opportunities as boys. Statistics can shed light on collective destinies but it should never be forgotten that their findings must be interpreted with due caution.

TABLE 1. Comparison of enrolment ratios of boys and girls at various ages

| States | Year | 6 years | | 8 years | | 10 years | |
|---|---|---|---|---|---|---|---|
| | | Boys | Girls | Boys | Girls | Boys | Girls |
| **AFRICA** | | | | | | | |
| *Eastern Africa* | | | | | | | |
| Burundi | 1969 | *31.0* | *18.6* | *36.7* | *18.6* | *33.6* | *16.1* |
| Mauritius | 1968 | 95.8 | 91.5 | 98.6 | 95.8 | *94.1* | *87.4* |
| Mozambique | 1966 | *39.4* | *19.7* | *55.6* | *32.8* | *50.7* | *30.4* |
| *Middle Africa* | | | | | | | |
| Central African Empire | 1970 | *73.5* | *42.0* | *95.6* | *51.4* | *68.2* | *31.7* |
| Chad | 1969 | *21.9* | *9.8* | *31.5* | *10.9* | *30.2* | *8.4* |
| United Republic of Cameroon | 1971 | *82.7* | *65.8* | *85.7* | *67.9* | *83.7* | *63.1* |
| *Southern Africa* | | | | | | | |
| Botswana | 1971 | 19.1 | 21.6 | | | 56.3 | 54.3 |
| Swaziland | 1970 | 35.4 | 37.7 | 61.9 | 66.8 | 73.9 | 72.2 |
| *Western Africa* | | | | | | | |
| Benin | 1968 | *38.9* | *17.0* | *41.7* | *18.2* | *39.0* | *15.9* |
| Gambia | 1971 | *31.6* | *17.9* | *31.8* | *17.3* | *39.5* | *16.0* |
| Togo | 1971 | *69.2* | *39.1* | *76.9* | *43.2* | *83.2* | *35.1* |
| Upper Volta | 1967 | 6.9 | 4.6 | *14.6* | *8.9* | *12.9* | *7.5* |
| **AMERICA** | | | | | | | |
| *Caribbean* | | | | | | | |
| Cuba | 1971 | 120.9 | 124.6 | 125.9 | 126.4 | 104.2 | 105.2 |
| *Middle America* | | | | | | | |
| Costa Rica | 1972 | 53.6 | 56.0 | 95.2 | 95.2 | 94.5 | 94.6 |
| Guatemala | 1969 | 6.6 | 5.7 | *60.3* | *52.2* | *64.1* | *52.4* |
| Panama | 1971 | 52.7 | 55.4 | 95.6 | 97.2 | 96.8 | 97.5 |
| *Temperate South America* | | | | | | | |
| Argentina | 1969 | 99.1 | 101.4 | 96.9 | 101.1 | 96.5 | 99.3 |
| *Tropical South America* | | | | | | | |
| Ecuador | 1969 | 56.0 | 58.4 | 81.9 | 80.3 | 81.8 | 78.8 |
| Peru | 1965 | 48.7 | 47.2 | *74.5* | *67.3* | *83.3* | *73.6* |
| *Northern America* | | | | | | | |
| United States | 1969 | 98.0 | 98.4 | 99.0 | 100.0 | 99.0 | 99.5 |

| 12 years | | 15 years | | 16 years | | 18 years | | 20 years | |
|---|---|---|---|---|---|---|---|---|---|
| Boys | Girls | Boys | Girls | Boys | Girls | Boys | Girls | Boys | Girl |
| *26.8* | *9.8* | *9.9* | *2.5* | *5.6* | *1.4* | *2.4* | *0.4* | *1.0* | *0.1* |
| *75.0* | *60.7* | *35.0* | *26.2* | *32.8* | *19.1* | *22.5* | *9.4* | *4.9* | *1.7* |
| *50.6* | *13.5* | *2.4* | *1.3* | *2.4* | *2.3* | *1.8* | *0.8* | *0.9* | *0.3* |
| *51.2* | *23.3* | *20.7* | *7.8* | *11.0* | *3.0* | 5.7 | 1.2 | 2.0 | 0.3 |
| *28.3* | *6.0* | *10.6* | *2.0* | 5.6 | 0.7 | 2.9 | 0.3 | 1.1 | 0.0 |
| *79.9* | *54.3* | *42.0* | *23.1* | *24.8* | *11.7* | *15.6* | *4.9* | 4.9 | 1.0 |
| *52.6* | *60.6* | 40.3 | 42.2 | *36.9* | *28.7* | *14.3* | *7.9* | 5.4 | 1.3 |
| 66.9 | 66.1 | *52.6* | *42.5* | *49.2* | *33.0* | *28.1* | *12.4* | *9.8* | *4.2* |
| *28.5* | *12.6* | *11.8* | *5.0* | 8.2 | 3.3 | 4.7 | 1.7 | 2.2 | 0.8 |
| *44.0* | *14.4* | *16.2* | *5.8* | *11.3* | *4.5* | *6.2* | *1.1* | *0.0* | *0.0* |
| *75.0* | *28.0* | *38.5* | *12.2* | 13.5 | 3.5 | 5.3 | 1.0 | 2.3 | 0.6 |
| *15.4* | *4.7* | *9.6* | *1.9* | *7.0* | *0.8* | *3.9* | *0.5* | *0.9* | *0.1* |
| 86.0 | 82.7 | 42.8 | 38.8 | 28.9 | 24.1 | 9.4 | 8.7 | 6.2 | 4.7 |
| 86.5 | 84.2 | 41.9 | 42.4 | 34.5 | 36.6 | 28.3 | 25.9 | 18.4 | 14.0 |
| *56.8* | *42.6* | *20.6* | *16.0* | *16.3* | *10.9* | 9.3 | 5.7 | 6.6 | 2.7 |
| 91.6 | 91.9 | 61.3 | 58.9 | 50.0 | 49.3 | 34.7 | 36.5 | 18.6 | 18.1 |
| 93.7 | 96.3 | 40.0 | 43.7 | 31.8 | 35.9 | 19.2 | 19.9 | 12.1 | 12.5 |
| *73.6* | *66.4* | 36.5 | 31.0 | *33.3* | *26.8* | 18.3 | 13.7 | *12.0* | *6.4* |
| *84.2* | *70.2* | *64.0* | *43.3* | *51.8* | *33.6* | *32.9* | *19.8* | *20.4* | *13.1* |
| 99.0 | 98.5 | 97.0 | 96.0 | 94.0 | 92.0 | 67.0 | 65.0 | 50.0 | 28.0 |

TABLE 1 *(continued)*

| States | Year | 6 years | | 8 years | | 10 years | |
|---|---|---|---|---|---|---|---|
| | | Boys | Girls | Boys | Girls | Boys | Girls |
| ASIA | | | | | | | |
| *East Asia* | | | | | | | |
| Japan | 1970 | 100.1 | 98.9 | 100.9 | 100.0 | 99.6 | 98.8 |
| Republic of Korea | 1971 | *81.0* | *76.8* | *103.4* | *97.9* | *106.0* | *98.4* |
| *Eastern South Asia* | | | | | | | |
| Malaysia | 1970 | 97.9 | 95.2 | 96.9 | 93.9 | *87.8* | *79.8* |
| *Middle South Asia* | | | | | | | |
| India | 1967 | *81.5* | *54.0* | *86.4* | *54.2* | *67.1* | *36.0* |
| *Western South Asia* | | | | | | | |
| Cyprus | 1972 | *69.8* | *79.7* | *77.0* | *69.9* | *78.0* | *73.4* |
| Jordan | 1971 | *37.4* | *27.4* | *58.9* | *47.2* | *54.8* | *44.7* |
| EUROPE | | | | | | | |
| *Eastern Europe* | | | | | | | |
| Bulgaria | 1971 | 4.4 | 4.7 | 97.1 | 97.3 | 96.3 | 96.7 |
| Hungary | 1972 | 96.1 | 95.8 | 96.2 | 97.1 | 94.2 | 95.8 |
| *Northern Europe* | | | | | | | |
| Sweden | 1969 | 1.0 | 1.7 | 100.4 | 101.0 | 99.5 | 99.3 |
| United Kingdom | 1970 | 100.1 | 99.9 | 98.8 | 99.1 | 101.2 | 101.7 |
| *Southern Europe* | | | | | | | |
| Greece | 1970 | 101.7 | 102.9 | 98.5 | 98.4 | 95.8 | 93.9 |
| Portugal | 1970 | 20.9 | 22.5 | 101.8 | 103.4 | 98.9 | 101.0 |
| Spain | 1970 | 109.7 | 114.2 | 102.7 | 104.2 | 105.2 | 104.1 |
| Yugoslavia | 1970 | *0.0* | *0.0* | 96.1 | 94.5 | 99.5 | 96.3 |
| *Western Europe* | | | | | | | |
| Belgium | 1968 | 100.9 | 100.3 | 99.8 | 99.9 | 101.5 | 100.5 |
| France | 1967 | 99.9 | 100.7 | 100.3 | 100.5 | 97.8 | 98.9 |
| Germany (Federal Republic of) | 1970 | 60.0 | 63.9 | 100.6 | 100.9 | 101.1 | 101.9 |
| Netherlands | 1971 | 72.1 | 72.9 | 97.9 | 99.6 | 95.7 | 99.5 |
| OCEANIA | | | | | | | |
| New Zealand | 1971 | 99.1 | 98.0 | 99.1 | 99.5 | 101.1 | 101.2 |

*Source:* Unesco Office of Statistics, *The Dimension of School Enrolment. A Study of Enrolment Ratios in the World,* p. 97–129, Paris, 1975 (Current Studies and Research in Statistics, CSR-E-16).

| 12 years | | 15 years | | 16 years | | 18 years | | 20 years | |
|---|---|---|---|---|---|---|---|---|---|
| Boys | Girls | Boys | Girls | Boys | Girls | Boys | Girls | Boys | Girls |
| 99.4 | 98.6 | 82.2 | 81.5 | 78.2 | 78.4 | 36.1 | 21.8 | 22.8 | 5.5 |
| 63.6 | 55.9 | 59.0 | 40.0 | 47.9 | 31.5 | 27.8 | 14.5 | 10.6 | 4.6 |
| 81.0 | 58.7 | 25.8 | 18.7 | 26.0 | 17.6 | 7.3 | 4.2 | 4.3 | 2.1 |
| 53.1 | 24.3 | 34.3 | 12.5 | 26.6 | 8.9 | 14.8 | 4.5 | 6.9 | 1.9 |
| 81.8 | 77.7 | 52.7 | 55.3 | 50.8 | 51.5 | 17.3 | 12.5 | 1.4 | 0.9 |
| 44.7 | 43.3 | 33.6 | 28.1 | 31.8 | 21.8 | 24.8 | 12.2 | 8.5 | 3.0 |
| 96.2 | 95.8 | 81.1 | 80.7 | 66.3 | 68.3 | 31.3 | 33.5 | 10.0 | 17.5 |
| 96.4 | 96.9 | 78.6 | 61.7 | 72.2 | 53.3 | 12.6 | 9.7 | 9.0 | 7.6 |
| 98.5 | 99.9 | 91.5 | 93.8 | 71.5 | 70.8 | 44.9 | 39.9 | 22.3 | 23.4 |
| 99.9 | 100.8 | 73.4 | 74.1 | 40.8 | 40.1 | 22.3 | 17.4 | 19.4 | 11.6 |
| 85.2 | 74.5 | 63.1 | 47.8 | 55.8 | 43.7 | 36.9 | 16.6 | 24.6 | 9.8 |
| 83.9 | 79.9 | 30.5 | 25.3 | 25.2 | 20.1 | 21.4 | 16.3 | 14.5 | 11.3 |
| 98.7 | 93.4 | 40.6 | 30.5 | 33.6 | 24.3 | 24.7 | 14.0 | 21.3 | 11.4 |
| 98.0 | 87.3 | 76.7 | 65.8 | 61.1 | 49.2 | 50.2 | 39.9 | 21.8 | 18.1 |
| 98.9 | 98.2 | 78.1 | 77.9 | 68.2 | 64.2 | 42.1 | 35.1 | 24.0 | 15.2 |
| 96.7 | 98.1 | 58.7 | 65.8 | 49.6 | 56.6 | 27.3 | 28.7 | 14.2 | 12.2 |
| 101.3 | 101.2 | 99.8 | 99.0 | 100.0 | 92.8 | 60.5 | 37.6 | 20.4 | 13.2 |
| 94.7 | 98.7 | 88.8 | 79.0 | 70.7 | 54.7 | 38.1 | 20.6 | 22.2 | 9.3 |
| 102.8 | 100.7 | 87.7 | 84.7 | 60.5 | 54.5 | 19.5 | 18.1 | 16.5 | 10.0 |

TABLE 2. Values of the ratio:

$$\frac{\text{total enrolments (primary + secondary + higher)}}{\text{population 6-29 years}} \times 100$$

| Country | Year | Boys | Girls |
|---|---|---|---|
| Argentina | 1968 | 45.6 | 46.3 |
| Belgium | 1968 | 56.2 | 53.2 |
| Benin | 1968 | 18.1 | 7.9 |
| Botswana | 1971 | 26.8 | 28.6 |
| Bulgaria | 1971 | 46.0 | 46.1 |
| Burundi | 1969 | 15.5 | 7.0 |
| Central African Empire | 1968 | 32.9 | 13.4 |
| Chad | 1969 | 14.7 | 4.1 |
| Costa Rica | 1964 | 45.8 | 43.5 |
| Cuba | 1965 | 41.5 | 41.0 |
| Cyprus | 1971 | 39.6 | 37.1 |
| Ecuador | 1969 | 42.6 | 38.7 |
| France | 1967 | 50.8 | 52.7 |
| Gambia | 1971 | 18.1 | 7.5 |
| Germany (Federal Republic of) | 1970 | 59.4 | 54.6 |
| Greece | 1969 | 50.6 | 42.7 |
| Guatemala | 1968 | 26.9 | 21.0 |
| Hungary | 1972 | 42.3 | 38.2 |
| India | 1967 | 39.3 | 21.1 |
| Japan | 1970 | 48.8 | 44.4 |
| Jordan | 1965 | 39.5 | 24.9 |
| Korea | 1968 | 51.0 | 43.9 |
| Kuwait | 1971 | 28.8 | 35.5 |
| Malaysia | 1968 | 44.9 | 38.7 |
| Mauritius | 1968 | 48.6 | 41.4 |
| Mozambique | 1966 | 19.7 | 10.1 |
| Netherlands | 1970 | 52.4 | 46.9 |
| New Zealand | 1971 | 62.0 | 59.1 |
| Panama | 1971 | 52.8 | 52.1 |
| Peru | 1965 | 48.6 | 39.1 |
| Portugal | 1970 | 42.4 | 37.5 |
| Spain | 1969 | 48.3 | 42.4 |
| Swaziland | 1970 | 39.6 | 34.5 |
| Sweden | 1969 | 49.9 | 48.1 |
| Togo | 1970 | 38.2 | 15.9 |
| United Kingdom | 1970 | 56.6 | 54.3 |
| United Republic of Cameroon | 1971 | 42.6 | 29.8 |
| Upper Volta | 1969 | 42.8 | 34.1 |
| Yugoslavia | 1970 | 47.3 | 41.4 |

*Source:* Unesco Office of Statistics, op. cit., p. 52-3.

TABLE 3. Enrolment ratios by age-group and by sex in twenty-three regions of the world, 19/3[1]

| Region[2] | 6–11 years | | 12–17 years | | 18–23 years | | 6–23 years | |
|---|---|---|---|---|---|---|---|---|
| | Boys | Girls | Boys | Girls | Boys | Girls | Boys | Girls |
| Eastern Africa | 52.5 | 41.0 | 33.0 | 19.8 | 4.7 | 1.5 | 33.1 | 23.3 |
| Middle Africa | 77.9 | 54.5 | 51.6 | 26.5 | 6.9 | 2.1 | 49.5 | 30.7 |
| Northern Africa | 69.5 | 45.4 | 42.3 | 23.0 | 16.3 | 7.2 | 46.3 | 27.8 |
| Southern Africa | 82.4 | 85.6 | 73.6 | 70.4 | 10.1 | 4.4 | 59.6 | 58.0 |
| Western Africa | 43.8 | 29.9 | 28.9 | 15.9 | 5.5 | 1.8 | 28.6 | 17.7 |
| Caribbean | 85.1 | 86.8 | 60.3 | 59.4 | 16.5 | 12.1 | 58.6 | 57.4 |
| Middle America | 84.5 | 83.1 | 57.8 | 45.9 | 17.5 | 7.9 | 57.8 | 50.6 |
| Temperate South America | 98.0 | 98.1 | 69.7 | 73.3 | 27.4 | 23.6 | 66.6 | 66.7 |
| Tropical South America | 70.2 | 71.6 | 56.4 | 54.1 | 23.6 | 21.1 | 52.8 | 51.8 |
| Northern America | 99.3 | 99.3 | 94.8 | 95.2 | 51.1 | 45.0 | 81.4 | 79.4 |
| Japan | 100.0 | 100.0 | 94.6 | 94.7 | 29.8 | 14.9 | 74.4 | 69.0 |
| Other East Asia | 97.9 | 97.8 | 70.7 | 58.1 | 18.0 | 9.8 | 65.4 | 58.2 |
| Eastern South Asia | 70.8 | 64.9 | 43.0 | 34.8 | 10.4 | 7.1 | 45.5 | 39.3 |
| Middle South Asia | 70.0 | 43.8 | 35.0 | 17.4 | 8.5 | 2.7 | 41.8 | 23.9 |
| Western South Asia | 77.9 | 57.4 | 53.9 | 31.8 | 17.9 | 6.9 | 53.5 | 35.2 |
| Eastern Europe | 91.8 | 91.3 | 79.7 | 81.3 | 17.0 | 19.1 | 60.7 | 61.8 |
| Northern Europe | 97.7 | 98.3 | 81.6 | 82.7 | 28.6 | 19.7 | 70.8 | 68.6 |
| Southern Europe | 96.7 | 97.2 | 73.4 | 65.6 | 34.5 | 23.3 | 69.5 | 63.3 |
| Western Europe | 95.3 | 95.9 | 87.1 | 88.8 | 34.9 | 23.3 | 73.3 | 70.5 |
| Australia and New Zealand | 99.7 | 99.1 | 79.8 | 79.5 | 24.5 | 16.2 | 68.7 | 66.0 |
| Melanesia | 46.8 | 36.3 | 45.6 | 24.1 | 7.6 | 1.6 | 35.8 | 23.0 |
| Polynesia and Micronesia | 93.4 | 96.8 | 91.5 | 85.9 | 12.9 | 10.0 | 70.2 | 68.3 |
| USSR | 82.0 | 82.0 | 77.3 | 82.5 | 22.8 | 25.2 | 60.4 | 63.1 |

1. Ratio between the enrolment of the given age-group and the population of the same age-group.
2. The list of countries and territories within each region may be found in Appendix II.
Source: Unesco Office of Statistics, Trends and Projections of Enrolment by Level of Education and by Age, p. 47–50, Paris, 1978 (Current Studies and Research in Statistics, CSR-E-21).

TABLE 4. Gross enrolment ratios in twenty-three regions of the world, by level of education and by sex, 1975[1]

| Region | 1st level 6–11 years | | 2nd level 12–17 years | | 3rd level 18–23 years | | Total 6–23 years | |
|---|---|---|---|---|---|---|---|---|
| | Boys | Girls | Boys | Girls | Boys | Girls | Boys | Girls |
| Eastern Africa | 74.6 | 54.2 | 10.4 | 5.7 | 0.7 | 0.2 | 33.4 | 23.5 |
| Middle Africa | 109.6 | 71.5 | 20.3 | 9.3 | 1.4 | 0.2 | 50.1 | 31.1 |
| Northern Africa | 82.1 | 52.4 | 35.1 | 18.6 | 7.6 | 3.1 | 46.6 | 28.0 |
| Southern Africa | 132.3 | 132.3 | 19.4 | 18.5 | 6.0 | 2.1 | 60.1 | 58.6 |
| Western Africa | 61.6 | 40.5 | 12.3 | 5.1 | 0.9 | 0.2 | 29.0 | 18.0 |
| Caribbean | 108.3 | 107.2 | 41.1 | 41.5 | 8.9 | 7.3 | 59.1 | 58.0 |
| Middle America | 110.5 | 103.9 | 32.2 | 24.2 | 10.5 | 3.7 | 57.8 | 50.6 |
| Temperate South America | 135.4 | 134.9 | 39.5 | 45.3 | 20.1 | 15.8 | 67.2 | 67.7 |
| Tropical South America | 108.6 | 108.3 | 22.2 | 22.2 | 10.2 | 7.6 | 52.8 | 51.8 |
| Northern America | 121.1 | 120.6 | 80.3 | 82.8 | 46.6 | 38.7 | 81.4 | 79.4 |
| Japan | 100.2 | 100.0 | 95.2 | 95.5 | 29.0 | 14.2 | 74.4 | 69.0 |
| Other East Asia | 108.4 | 108.5 | 66.7 | 52.3 | 10.3 | 4.1 | 65.5 | 58.2 |
| Eastern South Asia | 89.5 | 80.2 | 26.7 | 20.3 | 4.3 | 3.8 | 45.9 | 39.7 |
| Middle South Asia | 75.7 | 48.9 | 40.0 | 18.6 | 4.4 | 1.6 | 44.6 | 26.0 |
| Western South Asia | 95.1 | 68.8 | 41.7 | 21.6 | 8.3 | 3.3 | 53.7 | 35.3 |
| Eastern Europe | 143.7 | 142.8 | 35.9 | 39.6 | 11.9 | 12.8 | 60.7 | 61.8 |
| Northern Europe | 110.8 | 110.3 | 94.0 | 94.0 | 19.0 | 12.7 | 76.6 | 74.5 |
| Southern Europe | 102.0 | 99.5 | 82.2 | 73.7 | 20.0 | 13.1 | 69.9 | 63.7 |
| Western Europe | 99.3 | 98.4 | 97.4 | 96.0 | 19.9 | 13.2 | 73.4 | 70.6 |
| Australia and New Zealand | 114.7 | 112.6 | 76.6 | 77.1 | 23.0 | 15.4 | 72.1 | 69.4 |
| Melanesia | 74.0 | 49.6 | 16.1 | 8.5 | 3.7 | 1.0 | 35.8 | 23.0 |
| Polynesia and Micronesia | 143.4 | 140.3 | 44.7 | 44.2 | 4.2 | 3.4 | 70.2 | 68.3 |
| USSR | 141.1 | 140.4 | 32.5 | 39.5 | 16.8 | 17.8 | 60.4 | 63.1 |

1. Ratio between enrolment for a given level of education and the school age population at this level, in this case 6–11 years, 12–17 years, 18–23 years and 6–23 years respectively (ratios above 100% indicate the presence of pupils whose age does not correspond to that which has been officially selected).
Source: Unesco Office of Statistics, Trends and Projections of Enrolment by Level of Education and by Age, op. cit., p. 56–9.

TABLE 5. Disparities in male and female enrolment ratios at the age of 16 in France, by occupational category of parents

| Occupational category | Enrolment ratio at 16 | | | Enrolment ratio in upper secondary education—'long' cycle | | | Enrolment ratio in upper secondary education—'short' cycle | | |
|---|---|---|---|---|---|---|---|---|---|
| | Boys | Girls | Difference | Boys | Girls | Difference | Boys | Girls | Difference |
| Higher professional | 98.6 | 96.9 | —1.7 | 85.5 | 82.4 | —3.1 | 4.2 | 7.8 | +3.6 |
| Middle-level professional | 87.6 | 92.3 | +4.7 | 57.1 | 61.0 | +3.9 | 18.2 | 21.7 | +3.5 |
| Office-workers | 82.6 | 82.4 | —0.2 | 32.4 | 41.2 | +8.8 | 36.6 | 29.8 | —6.8 |
| Small trades and shopkeepers | 76.7 | 86.8 | +10.1 | 44.7 | 55.8 | +11.1 | 22.0 | 18.4 | —3.6 |
| Farmers | 74.0 | 83.6 | +9.6 | 38.1 | 42.1 | +4.0 | 27.7 | 29.0 | +1.3 |
| Farm-workers | 75.5 | 80.4 | +4.9 | 28.7 | 31.5 | +2.8 | 35.1 | 29.3 | —5.8 |
| Skilled workers | 72.3 | 80.5 | +8.2 | 29.7 | 36.7 | +7.0 | 32.6 | 32.1 | —0.5 |
| Semi-skilled workers | 59.0 | 72.5 | +13.5 | 17.9 | 27.7 | +9.8 | 33.9 | 35.1 | +1.2 |
| TOTAL | 74.8 | 81.6 | +6.8 | 35.8 | 41.9 | +6.1 | 28.5 | 28.3 | —0.2 |

*Source: Les jeunes et l'emploi*, p. 200, Paris, Presses Universitaires de France, 1975 (Cahiers du Centre d'Études de l'Emploi, 7).

TABLE 6. Percentage of female enrolments: evolution between 1965 and 1975

| Region | First level | | | Second level | | | Third level | | |
|---|---|---|---|---|---|---|---|---|---|
| | 1965 | 1970 | 1975 | 1965 | 1970 | 1975 | 1965 | 1970 | 1975 |
| Eastern Africa | 38 | 40 | 42 | 31 | 33 | 35 | 17 | 19 | 21 |
| Middle Africa | 34 | 38 | 40 | 22 | 26 | 32 | 8 | 10 | 15 |
| Northern Africa | 37 | 37 | 38 | 27 | 30 | 34 | 20 | 24 | 28 |
| Southern Africa | 50 | 50 | 50 | 47 | 48 | 49 | 26 | 25 | 27 |
| Western Africa | 38 | 38 | 40 | 26 | 28 | 29 | 13 | 14 | 18 |
| Caribbean | 49 | 49 | 49 | 51 | 50 | 50 | 44 | 47 | 45 |
| Middle America | 48 | 48 | 48 | 40 | 40 | 42 | 20 | 23 | 25 |
| Temperate South America | 49 | 49 | 49 | 53 | 53 | 53 | 39 | 42 | 43 |
| Tropical South America | 49 | 49 | 49 | 47 | 48 | 50 | 30 | 36 | 43 |
| Northern America | 49 | 49 | 49 | 50 | 50 | 50 | 39 | 41 | 45 |
| Japan | 49 | 49 | 49 | 49 | 49 | 49 | 25 | 28 | 32 |
| Other East Asia | 48 | 48 | 48 | 37 | 39 | 42 | 26 | 25 | 28 |
| Eastern South Asia | 46 | 47 | 47 | 39 | 40 | 42 | 46 | 46 | 46 |
| Middle South Asia | 36 | 36 | 38 | 24 | 28 | 30 | 21 | 22 | 25 |
| Western South Asia | 38 | 39 | 41 | 29 | 31 | 33 | 24 | 24 | 28 |
| Eastern Europe | 49 | 49 | 49 | 40 | 51 | 51 | 39 | 45 | 51 |
| Northern Europe | 49 | 49 | 49 | 48 | 48 | 49 | 32 | 36 | 39 |
| Southern Europe | 48 | 48 | 48 | 41 | 44 | 46 | 32 | 36 | 39 |
| Western Europe | 49 | 49 | 49 | 47 | 48 | 49 | 31 | 35 | 39 |
| Australia and New Zealand | 49 | 49 | 48 | 48 | 48 | 49 | 31 | 34 | 39 |
| Melanesia | 40 | 38 | 39 | 26 | 30 | 33 | — | 17 | 20 |
| Polynesia and Micronesia | 47 | 48 | 48 | 45 | 47 | 48 | 36 | 45 | 44 |
| USSR | 49 | 49 | 49 | 54 | 55 | 54 | 44 | 49 | 50 |

*Source:* International Conference on Education (36th session, Geneva, 30 August to 8 September 1977), *Development of School Enrolment: World and Regional Statistical Trends and Projections 1960–2000*, p. 66–70, report prepared by the Unesco Office of Statistics, Paris, July 1977 (Unesco doc. ED/BIE/CONFINED/36/4 Ref. 2).

TABLE 7. Number of countries by enrolment ratio for the 6–23 age-group

| Enrolment ratio | In 1965 | | In 1975 | |
|---|---|---|---|---|
| | Boys | Girls | Boys | Girls |
| Under 20% | 20 | 38 | 9 | 27 |
| From 20% to 40% | 34 | 28 | 24 | 24 |
| From 40% to 60% | 33 | 28 | 43 | 33 |
| Over 60% | 8 | ... | 20 | 11 |

PART TWO

# THE SCHOOL CAREER
# OF GIRLS AND BOYS

*The findings set forth in Part One should not blind the reader to the risks of inter-regional and inter-country comparisons. In some countries compulsory schooling lasts nine or ten years, in others four or five and in a few there is no compulsory schooling at all. Some pupils go to school for 170 days a year, others for 220; classes in primary education may cover six hours a day, or no more than three. The curricula may attach little or a great deal of importance to motivating activities and observation, to literature or to mathematics, and so forth. Although it is idle to hope for perfect comparability, comparisons are a worthwhile means of stimulating research and formulating hypotheses.*

*The advantage of a comparative study of the school career of girls and of boys in a particular country is that it avoids the hazards inherent in the diversity of systems, since it sets out to examine differences in treatment between the two sexes in a given socio-cultural and educational context. Once past the initial barrier — admission to a school — what happens to girls during their educational career? How, compared with boys, do they pursue their studies? It should be borne in mind that we do not have available complete statistical data for a fully satisfactory analysis of these problems.*

## METHODOLOGICAL CONSIDERATIONS

There may well be disagreement as to how the phenomena covered by the term 'wastage' should be measured or interpreted, but most people tend to agree over the basic facts. In many countries of the world, for example, some children leave school once and for all before they have completed a particular course of education. They are 'drop-outs' because the interruption of schooling is not temporary, as in the case of absence due to illness or seasonal occupations.

Moreover, when the study cycle is organized into self-contained stages, each with its own curriculum usually corresponding to a school year though sometimes to a course, a certain number of pupils are obliged to begin the year afresh; these we call 'repeaters'.

'Wastage' in education is a consequence of the combined impact of 'drop-outs' and 'repeaters'.

What tools are available to pinpoint and measure wastage in education? The only rigorous method would involve collecting individualized data so that the school career of each pupil could be followed up and the information fed into a computer, but this would require considerable financial and human resources and no such information is available.

As a matter of fact, the revelation of wastage was a by-product of early efforts to apply planning techniques to education regarded not at the classroom or school level but at the level of the state. The first macro-analyses made it necessary to examine the educational statistics pertaining to a particular level of instruction and to changes from one course and one school year to another, and it emerged that pupil numbers diminished in a significant and unexpected way. This led to talk of 'apparent cohorts', 'enrolment losses', 'wastage' and 'educational rejects'. The statistical observation of the evolution or enrolments revealed that the set of pupils

45

in each stage of an educational cycle — generally speaking a school year — never formed a completely homogeneous group but were made up of two categories of pupils: 'newcomers', that is, pupils new to the particular content and course in question but not to the school, and 'old' pupils who had already taken the course, usually in the previous year.

Pupil promotion or the apparent cohort is the most elementary symptom of wastage: it provides information on certain hitherto somewhat neglected phenomena, and in particular on one aspect of school zoning, namely changes in the number of classrooms from one course to another; but it does not enable us to assess the actual wastage since it is simply the outcome of a series of pupil movements from one class to another and from one year to another whose magnitude is unknown.

In reality, the 'apparent cohort' and the three indicators which measure pupil movements — promotion, repetition and drop-out — highlight quite different phenomena, even though there are definite connections between them. For example, planners are well aware of a certain form of repetition which affects the terminal classes of study cycles when access to the next cycle is limited, but there is no doubt that, even though boys and girls compete, the real reasons for drop-out or repetition are difficult to determine.

By examining the number of repeaters among the pupils, it is possible to calculate the three rates (promotion, repetition, drop-out) for each grade so as to establish a more satisfactory statistical comparison between girls and boys at the various stages of an educational cycle and at different periods. When based on a representative sample and filled out with further data on individual characteristics, a comparison of this kind should clarify the factors governing success and failure at school.

These rates, expressing changes from one school year to the next or based on some shorter or longer period of time, make it possible to estimate various forms of wastage. It is possible to reconstitute the educational destiny of a cohort of 1,000 pupils enrolled in the first year of primary education by employing the graphic technique known as the 'Lexis flow diagrams' and by assuming that this group of pupils will advance through the educational cycle in accordance with previously observed rates of promotion, repetition and drop-out. This produces probabilities from which promotion without repetition, promotion with repetition, and drop-out may be deduced for each stage of the cycle in question.

Another method of approach is to calculate school life expectancy. On the basis of enrolment broken down by age, it is assumed that the pupil's chances are determined by the observed situation in a given year and from this the probable amount of time he will spend in the school system is deduced.

These diverse means of apprehending the pupil's educational career will be utilized in this study for the comparison between boys and girls. They do not claim to reflect actual patterns of behaviour, a fact that is particularly regrettable inasmuch as girls' schooling, though still behind, is changing and expanding rapidly in all countries of the world. It is therefore difficult to assume that future patterns will be the same for both sexes.

## COMPARATIVE PROGRESSION OF MALE AND FEMALE PUPILS IN REGIONS WITH LOWEST ENROLMENT

When examining Table 8[1] the first thing to note is that a very sharp drop in pupil numbers, affecting both boys and girls, often occurs between the first and second year of primary education;[2] by the fifth year, less than 50% of the initial intake remain. This phenomenon is all the more serious inasmuch as by no means all children attend school.

Boys are better placed than girls in all the regions of Africa and Asia, and in Middle America; in the other regions of Latin America, girls outnumber boys at all levels though by very little in Tropical South America.

The differentiation increases from one grade to the next so that the widest gaps are always to be found at the end of the cycle: it cannot be contented that the initial barrier ensures subsequent equality of pupil progression for those admitted to school. We may also observe that, in the second year, girls are clearly worse off in only two regions, Middle Africa and Middle South Asia. Lastly, it should not be forgotten that Table 8 sets forth average values only: not all countries in a particular region have reached the same level of enrolment.

Table 9 shows that girls decrease in number more rapidly than all pupils together; thus the proportion of boys tends to increase as the level of education rises. When girls happen to progress as quickly or more quickly than boys, this is only in the early stages of schooling and never after the fourth year. There is clearly a need to analyse this phenomenon more precisely, taking into considera-

1. Except in Northern Africa, Western South Asia and Temperate South America.
2. Tables referred to in Part Two will be found on pages 63–73.

tion the age of the pupils, their geographical origin and their family background.

This kind of information on the comparative evolution of male and female pupil numbers by grade is but rarely circulated, particularly where the second level of education is concerned, for want of a satisfactory interpretation. Nevertheless, it is very useful since

knowledge of how the pupils progress from class to class in a course of education that extends over a given period and follows set procedures (rules of admission, grading, promotion and so forth) which characterize the system in question provides a very significant indication of educational supply. Studies conducted by the IEDES[1] on the performance of education have already demonstrated the feasibility of utilizing the size of classes to analyse, without much risk of error, the pupil's educational prospects in terms of classrooms, teachers and hours of instruction.[2]

It would be particularly enlightening to analyse the impact of educational supply on the number of girls attending school since study on the evolution of female pupil numbers can pinpoint the level at which sexual differentiation is strongest and then explore the conditions of admission and enrolment to find its causes.

PUPIL FLOWS IN THE EDUCATION SYSTEM:
COMPARISON OF PROMOTION, REPETITION
AND DROP-OUT AMONG GIRLS AND BOYS

Changes in teaching methods together with the economic analysis of education systems by planners have stimulated the interest of teachers and education officials in the problem of repeaters and drop-outs. The problem of repeaters has been thoroughly examined by educators and psychologists, some of whom have flatly condemned it and substituted automatic promotion. As for drop-outs , of which there are a great number, more attention is now being paid to this problem, which is no longer a consequence of 'straightforward rejection by the teacher' but rather the result of a decision by the pupil or his family. In countries with compulsory schooling, drop-out, in theory, does not occur before the end of the compulsory period, when it constitutes the alternative to continuation of studies.

1. Institut d'Étude du Développement Économique et Social, University of Paris I, France.
2. Isabelle Deblé, 'La déperdition d'effectifs dans le Tiers Monde et ses ambiguïtés', *Revue Tiers-Monde* (Institut d'Étude du Développement Économique et Social, Paris), Vol. 15, No. 59/60, 1974, p. 557.

To simplify matters, it could be said that repetition is forced on families by the school whereas the decision to drop out is more likely to be taken by the pupil himself or by his family.

Data collected by the Unesco Office of Statistics (not all utilized here for fear of overburdening the text) have made it possible to calculate, for various years between 1970 and 1975, the rates of promotion, repetition and drop-out for primary school children of each sex per grade in forty-three countries from the various regions of the world (see Appendix VII). Comparing the promotion rate by sex in the first and fourth years of schooling, countries have been divided into three groups (Table 9) which gives rise to the following observations:

In the first year, the promotion rate for girls is often higher than that for boys (in twenty-five countries), but the situation changes when we turn to the fourth year of schooling (chosen because it enables more states to be compared): by this time girls are ahead in only sixteen countries.

The high promotion rate for girls is not restricted to countries with high enrolment: eighteen of the states concerned belong to Middle Africa, the Caribbean, Middle America, Tropical and Temperate South America, Eastern and Western South Asia.

In cases where the promotion rate for girls is lower than that for boys in the first year, it is also lower four years later.

Countries in Group 1 (see Table 10) i.e. with a higher promotion rate for girls, for the first year of schooling and subsequently in Group 3 (higher rate for boys) display from the start average or low promotion rates and hence very high wastage.

When countries move from Group 1 to Group 2 (equal promotion rates for boys and girls), this indicates little sexual differentiation in first-year promotion rates.

Most of the countries remaining in Group 1 show, whatever the year of study, high promotion rates and insignificant variations by sex.

Once admitted to primary school, and taking promotion as the criterion of success, girls tend to obtain rather better results than boys but, at this general level of analysis and especially in developing countries, gradually lose ground as the level of education rises.

These remarks, which are based on a single observation rather than on a time series, are not universally applicable. They do however counter the claim that, in the present system, boys always benefit from a higher rate of promotion.

As for interrelationships between promotion, repetition and dropout, we may note the following facts:

When the first-year promotion rate is higher for girls, many boys repeat or drop out: the initial situation is favourable to female enrolment.

The same holds true for countries with a higher fourth-year promotion rate for girls than for boys.

The opposite situation (higher promotion rate among boys) produces a similar effect: generally more repetition and drop-out among first-year girls. In cases where, at a later stage in the course, promotion acts in favour of boys, female drop-out rates are always higher but repetition rates remain high for all pupils as if, having reached the fourth year, they were trying hard to remain at school

A certain number of countries, mostly in Latin America, have very high or relatively high drop-out rates. It should be emphasized that these drop-outs seem much more closely related to faults in the school system than to the sex of the pupils.

When the female promotion rate gradually falls between the first and fourth years, this is usually because of drop-outs, suggesting that generally more girls drop out than boys, whether or not their repetition rate is higher or lower.

In the few cases where female promotion rates are higher in the fourth than in the first year, male repeaters are more numerous, indicating that more non-promoted girls than boys leave school.

A study on the situation in Africa has revealed that

in 8 countries, repetition rates were similar for boys and girls at the first grade; in 10 others, rates at this grade were higher for girls and in a further 7 they were higher for boys. On the other hand, the rate at the last grade was higher in 14 countries for boys than for girls while the opposite was the case in 8 countries. Although it is generally clear that boys repeat more often than girls, the situation is the reverse as regards drop-out: the drop-out rate is higher for girls in almost all countries, especially at the penultimate grade.[1]

All these data give the impression that, during the recent period under review, pupil progression measured in terms of promotion, repetition and drop-out rates is not the most significant factor in the differentiation of male and female pupils. It is true, as can be seen in Table 10, that equality during the school career is not assured in a good third of the countries considered and that girls

---

1. Unesco Office of Statistics, *Wastage in Primary Education in Africa; Statistical Study/Les déperditions scolaires dans l'enseignement primaire en Afrique; étude statistique*, p. 11, Paris, 1975 (Current Studies and Research in Statistics, CSR-E-11).

are placed at a disadvantage, but in this respect, as we shall see later, some progress appears to have been made. But comparison also suggests that girls get on better than boys when their recruitment is more selective: one must beware of excessive optimism.

Promotion, repetition and drop-out rates are not available for the second level of education. It would be instructive to be able to check whether they too diverge in terms of sex as the level of education rises, as happens between the first and fourth years of primary education. It would also be of interest to look for possible links —taking boys and girls separately— between the intensity of enrolment and the variables governing progress through the educational continuum.

Table 11 based on data recently published in various ministry of education yearbooks, provides a few examples of observed rates in secondary education in three African countries.

EDUCATION OF BOYS AND GIRLS: COMPARISON
BY THE 'RECONSTRUCTED COHORT' METHOD

Comparative studies on the primary schooling of girls and boys carried out by means of the 'reconstructed cohort' method,[1] have made it possible to present findings for fifty-nine countries (see Table 12).

They give rise to the following observations:

In twenty-one countries,[2] there is a very low probability of completing the study cycle for both boys and girls, even in the most recent period examined.

In twenty-four out of twenty-eight African countries, the results are to the advantage of boys with, on occasion, very considerable differences between the two sexes.

On the other hand, in the fourteen Latin American countries covered, half of which reveal the highest wastage of all (measured in this way), the probabilities always favour girls (or are almost the same as for boys) but differences between the sexes are not striking, except in Cuba.

Fifteen Asian countries follow patterns closer to those found in Africa: boys are more likely than girls to complete their primary education, and sometimes by a long way.

1. For an account of this method see Unesco Office of Statistics, op. cit., p. 115 et seq.
2. Brazil, Burma, Burundi, Central African Empire, Chad, Colombia, Dominican Republic, El Salvador, Gabon, Guatemala, India, Lesotho, Madagascar, Malawi, Nicaragua, Oman, Paraguay, Rwanda, Thailand, Tunisia and Zaire.

In Greece boys have the best results and in Portugal girls, but in both cases the difference is insignificant.

What conclusions can be drawn from this incomplete set of data, mainly focused on developing countries? On the whole, boys are more likely to complete primary education in three cases out of five; the other two cases give the advantage to girls, even when the general level of enrolment is far from satisfactory.

Table 12 provides information on the probability of completing the first level of education but no indication as to exactly when pupils repeat or drop out. Yet precise knowledge here would constitute one of the best ways of comparing the school carreer—even in reconstructed form—of boys and girls. For example, it would be quite possible for the total number of drop-outs by the end of the cycle to include fewer girls than boys but for the figures to follow a pattern whereby more girls than boys leave the system in the first year. It is essential for the comparative evaluation of male and female school careers to know the level of instruction attained by all those who drop out.

In Tunisia, for instance, 'the girls who leave school do so earlier than their male classmates: 45.2% of them drop out before the 6th year whereas 70% of boys manage to go beyond this level'.[1] The difference between the overall drop-out rates (9.3% and 7.7% respectively) is not enough on its own to account for the highly significant fact that girls are in a worse position at the moment of transition from the first to the second level of education.

COMPARISON OF BOYS' AND GIRLS' SCHOOL
LIFE EXPECTANCIES[2]

Our reason for presenting a further indicator of wastage is that it has the advantage, in so far as it is valid, of expressing the two aspects of enrolment: the chances of admission in the first place and the chances or more of less completing the course of studies. Our earlier remarks on methodology stated that its purpose is to calculate, using techniques borrowed from demographic analysis, the probable duration of schooling. Two values are worked out: the first, in relation to the total population, measures the difficulty of gaining access to education, whereas the second, based on the

1. Saïda Mahfoudh, 'Scolarisation et emploi féminins', *Revue Tunisienne des sciences de l'éducation* (Tunis), No. 6, 1977, p. 89–129.
2. The method of calculating this indicator is described in: Unesco Office of Statistics, *The Dimensions of School Enrolment. A Study of enrolment Ratios in the World*, p. 27–8, Paris, 1975 (Current Studies and Research in Statistics, CSR-E-16).

school population, concentrates on the pupil who has succeeded in entering the system and expresses the probable length of time he will remain in it.

Table 13 sets out the results by sex for each value, at the age of 7 years.

As regards school life expectancy in relation to the total population, the table reveals enormous differences between countries: if we compare, for instance, Upper Volta (in 1971) and the Federal Republic of Germany (in 1973) we find that in the former the school life expectancy (in years) for boys is 1.2 and for girls 0.7 whereas in the latter the figures are, respectively 12.6 and 12.0. The relation is 1 to 10.5 for boys and 1 to 24 for girls and signifies that a boy of 7 is likely to spend, on average, ten times more time at school in one country than in the other, and a girl twenty-four times more.

These disparities become less striking when we examine school life expectancy in relation to the school population. Taking the same example, we note that a German boy or girl pupil will spend, on average, a little less than twice the amount of time at school (12.6 years for boys, 12.0 years for girls, than his or her counterpart in Upper Volta (7.0 years for boys, 6.7 years for girls) and that the difference in school life expectancy by sex is, in relation to the school population, small in both cases.

This indicator confirms that the greatest discrimination arises at the moment of initial access to education. Once past this hurdle, some differences remain but their impact is less.

We shall conclude this section by taking a concrete example which, though based on quite a different methodology, illustrates the differences in probable duration of schooling between three African countries. In 1973, the Ministry of Education in Togo published a comparative study of the educational situation of girls in the Ivory Coast, Chad and Togo.[1] It emerges that the repetition rate in primary education in 1970 was in all cases higher for girls than for boys, though the difference was slight except in the penultimate year (39.5% for girls as against 25.1% for boys). The authors emphasized that the most significant point was the difference between the proportion of girls and boys in the first and last years of the cycle: in 1969/70, for example, 21.6% of Ivory Coast boys were to be found in the first year and 16.7% in the final year whereas the corresponding figures for girls were 25.6% and

---

1. Togo, Ministère de l'Éducation Nationale, Direction de la Planification, des Statistiques et de la Conjoncture, *La fille et l'école. Étude comparative de la situation scolaire des filles. Côte d'Ivoire Tchad, Togo*, Loué, 1973.

11.1% respectively. In Togo, likewise in 1969/70, 30.6% of boys and 24.3% of girls were in the first year and 12% of boys and 8.6% of girls in the final year of primary education.

Table 14 shows the school career of pupils in the last grade of the first level of education in the Ivory Coast and Togo as calculated in 1970.

Apart from the fact that there are far fewer girls than boys, we may observe that the girls who reach the final grade have, in both countries, spent more time at school owing to repetition. In consequence an appreciable number of these female pupils are aged 15 or over, a situation which means that they may enter into marriage and become mothers.

The study states that 'in the Ivory Coast, the school system is almost twice as selective for girls as for boys; in Togo, it is one-and-a-half times as selective'.

## EVOLUTION OF WASTAGE AMONG GIRL PUPILS

There are as yet few comprehensive and thorough studies on the progression of female enrolments. This is in fact a highly complex phenomenon whose causes extend far beyond the school itself.

Available statistical data have, however, made it possible to bring out certain past trends in the progression of female pupils by region during two periods of time five or ten years apart, by employing the 'apparent cohort' or 'reconstructed cohort' methods (see Table 6 above and Appendix VII).

In all regions considered pupil flows have increased for both boys and girls, yet although the gap between the sexes has narrowed in certain cases, the number of girls reaching the final grade is always lower (except in Latin America) than the number of boys. In Middle Africa the difference between female and male enrolments in the fifth grade of primary education has remained the same: in spite of efforts to increase overall enrolments, there has so far been no action to help girls catch up. In Northern Africa, enrolment trends have clearly stabilized to the advantage of boys. There has been little change in the comparative situation by sex in Western Africa but in Eastern Africa the number of girls at the end of the first level has distinctly improved. In Eastern South Asia there has been practically no change in the variations observed in these two periods except that the number of boys in the final grade of the cycle has increased. In Middle South Asia, on the other hand, there has been a more noticeable improvement in pupil progression in each year of the cycle, but gaps between boys and girls have remained much the same: there are still fewer girls than boys at the end of each grade.

Countries in Western South Asia form a special case: the number of pupils entering school has been increasing more slowly—a disturbing pointer for future trends—but the end-of-cycle difference in the number of girls and boys, though still favouring boys, has been considerably reduced.

In short, except for Latin America and provided that the data employed are reliable, changes in pupil numbers from one grade to the next have not really favoured girls. This comparison of two periods contains no really convincing evidence: the overall results bear witness to considerable efforts but girls have benefited very little from them.

When we analyse Table 12 which is based on the method of reconstructed cohorts for two periods some ten years apart, we may note that the general situation of girls at school has improved in twenty African and Asian countries.[1] Progress has been undeniable, but it cannot be said that girls make up for their initial handicap—admission to school in smaller numbers—by advancing more quickly though their course of studies. For the moment, most of them still face one difficulty after another. However, without expressing an unseemly optimism, a certain number of factors appear to have combined to reduce the wide disparity between boys and girls at the start of their school careers that was observed some ten years ago. A child's education takes a very long time and this is the most serious limitation encountered when analysing trends in order to detect meaningful facts.

Another way of coming to grips with the changes in patterns of schooling by sex is to compare promotion, repetition and drop-out rates for each class over a given period of time. This would be a major statistical undertaking which is beyond the possibilities of this study. We have limited ourselves to comparing with the aid of data supplied by the Unesco Office of Statistics—pupil flows in the first year of school, decisive for the child's education future, and in the fourth year, which many regard as the level from which the knowledge taught stands some chance of being retained.

The striking thing about the first year of school is the improved promotion of girls in almost all countries whatever the period under review. This however should not disguise the relative nature of the change. It is remarkable that, in all European countries replying to

1. Algeria, Benin, Central African Empire, Congo, Cyprus, India, Iraq, Jordan, Kuwait, Libyan, Arab Jamahiriya, Madagascar, Niger, Republic of Korea, Rwanda, Saudi Arabia, Swaziland, Syrian Arab Republic, Upper Volta, Zaire and Zambia.

the Unesco questionnaire, this rate of promotion for girls is always higher at both the beginning and end of the period in question. The same holds for Latin America but the rates are distinctly lower and both sexes show a general improvement.

As regards the fourth grade, we have already noted that higher female promotion rates became less common towards 1975. They nevertheless show signs of improvement during the period covered, a clear indication that the initial situation was hardly favourable to girls. In most cases the difference is small, with improvements taking place at the snail's pace characteristic of education systems.

## Variations in annual repetition and drop-out rates for girls

Improved promotion in the first year has in general reduced the number of repeaters and drop-outs. For the child at school, however, the most decisive course of action at this juncture is to drop out, since this immediately puts an end to all hopes of advancing to higher levels of study.

In Africa, even though the total number of drop-outs at the start of the school career appears to have fallen, there has in most cases been an increase in repeaters, indicating that educational prospects at the beginning of the school career have not really improved.

In Latin America, the chances of completing primary education are very severely limited from the start for both girls and boys, In almost all the Asian countries reviewed, there has been distinct progress for girls at the beginning of primary education. Changes in the fourth-year rates take on their full significance only when compared to those of the preceding years at school: they are even better—or at least equal—between the two periods but are not high enough to make up for earlier pupil losses. A cursory analysis reveals that variations by sex and from one period to the next are small but more detailed studies by country should be undertaken.

The overall percentage of girls at school should not conceal the serious inconsistencies in school attendance for each grade. Indeed, it would be very instructive to examine the proportion of girls enrolled in each grade of an educational cycle in each country. Unfortunately, the data needed for a general picture of the situation in this respect are not available.

However, with the help of the data bank of the Unesco Office of Statistics, we have managed to trace a certain amount of information for Africa in 1975 which indicates that the percentage of girls in the first and last grades of primary education often varies to a great extent. Even though primary education, by reducing sexual disparities, provides the best example of a 'more open' and more democratic system of schooling, the observed differences range from 6.4% to 17.1% according to country.

In spite of a process of selection observed throughout the period of schooling, these differences are still present in the second level of education, as Table 15 makes clear. In most cases, the proportion of girls falls as the level of instruction rises. On the rare occasions when it is higher in the final than in the fourth year (Mauritania, Niger), this is because the upper cycle of the second level is underdeveloped and enrolments are limited, thus producing misleading rates. In such cases the selection—often at the expense of girls—tends to strengthen the motivation of those chosen—more often than not a few dozen—who then retain their privileged status as they continue their studies.

Discrimination both in initial admission to school and throughout primary education produce great differences in the number of potential candidates for the higher levels, at least in several African and Asian countries.

As a result of all this it is difficult to advance an opinion on the evolution of wastage in regard to girls over the last few years in countries whose level of enrolment is a long way behind: there are too many gaps in our knowledge. There is no doubt that a methodology should be developed that takes into account the intensity of female enrolment and its repercussions on the behaviour patterns of both sexes, changes in teaching structures and their impact on the school career of boys and girls, the freedom of movement for pupils in a system subjected to strong political and financial constraints, and many other factors.

DISPARITIES BETWEEN GIRLS AND BOYS AT SCHOOL

Not much has been written on this subject. Our knowledge is piecemeal and often contradictory. Existing studies are mainly sociological and at present, as we shall see, quickly take on a polemical turn involving a particular socio-political view of history. Regrettably the collection of data and development of appropriate parameters are still not on a sufficiently regular basis to yield a precise account of the quantitative and qualitative participation of girls in what many authors call the largest industry of the century.

Here we shall merely raise a few questions that recent research makes it possible to formulate.

Most analyses of education start out by considering the situation of pupils within the system, with variables like nationality, ethnic background or sex regarded as of secondary importance. This approach implies a refusal to recognize that the human race is made up of two sexes and a determination to explain the behaviour of each solely in relation to the others. The only way of comparing the schooling of girls and boys is to employ another methodology based on a different view of the problem.

The fact is that wastage in education is an ambiguous concept which takes a variety of forms: drop-out with or without previous repetition and repetition once or several times without dropping out, either of which can take place at any point in the school career and at different ages without there necessarily being a link between them. The first step in comparing the school careers of boys and girls would be to see how these eventualities differ for each sex.

The outcome of the foregoing analysis is to highlight the following facts:

The pursuit of studies beyond compulsory schooling—or at least beyond the first level—depends greatly on whether instruction has or has not been made available to all children, both male and female.

Countries having difficulty in catering for all the children for whom they have more or less implicitly planned to provide education find themselves in one of two situations: (a) either the schools contain girls and boys in equal numbers (often the case in Latin America), or (b) girls are clearly outnumbered (as in many African and Asian countries)—in consequence differentiation by sex does not simply reflect levels of development that limit the expansion of education.

In countries with high enrolment, where compulsory schooling covers a sizeable proportion of the second level—generally termed 'lower secondary education'—two types of structures are often to be distinguished: the first displays clearly differentiated streams from the start, or from quite an early stage in the cycle, whereas the second offers a single stream and postpones the need to choose until near the end of compulsory schooling. 'The distinction must however be qualified, since in reality there are not so much two opposite groups as different series of intermediate situations.'[1] Thus, apart from the different patterns of education within the same stream already mentioned, another

---

1. Organisation for Economic Co-operation and Development (OECD), *Beyond Compulsory Schooling; Options and Changes in Upper Secondary Education*, p. 19, Paris, 1976.

form of differential schooling to which we shall return later, distinguishes girls from boys: unequal representation in the various options.

It is frequently asserted that restricting the intake of girls, about which we shall offer no opinion here, improves their chances of success in the subsequent course of studies. We have hardly any information on promotion rates in the various years of secondary education—potential indicators of success even though dependent on the system's intake capacity—or on the pass rates in examinations. We can, however, offer the following details: in the Ivory Coast, which has a higher enrolment than Upper Volta, girls perform better than boys throughout—except for the first year, which serves as a test or barrier for pupils attending a new school. In Upper Volta this does not happen until the upper cycle, and even then the pass rate in the final examination is higher for boys. Our research has revealed that the pass rate, that is, the relation between the number of candidates and the number of passes, is in many cases higher for girls than for boys, but it is most unfortunate that the two sexes do not have the same chance at the outset.[1]

Another point is that access to secondary education is related, even more for girls than for boys, to membership of a higher socio-economic and cultural milieu: their better pass rate in examinations could therefore be ascribed to their more cultured and prosperous background.

In developed countries with high enrolment, it is generally agreed that schooling is not differentiated according to sex.

Two strictly scientific research projects, whose results are worth mentioning, have been carried out in France. The first followed the school career up to 1972 of a cross-section of 20,000 pupils from the 1962 final class of primary education[2]—in 1961/62 both sexes were more or less equally represented in all courses—and made it possible to examine the various aspects of social background and success at school. The second, dating from 1965,[3] covered over 100,000 pupils aged 6–14 years in order to embrace the entire primary cycle plus the first years of secondary education which at the time were given over to observation and guidance.

1. Marie Eliou, 'Scolarisation et promotion féminines en Afrique', *Revue Tiers-Monde* (Institut d'Étude de Développement Économique et Social, Paris), Vol. 13, No. 49, 1972, p. 41–83.
2. The results of the survey are presented in a series of individual or joint articles by Alain Girard, Henri Bastide, Guy Pourcher and Paul Clerc, published in the journal *Population* (Institut National d'Études Démographiques, Paris) in 1962, 1963, 1964, 1966, 1969 and 1972.
3. Institut National d'Études Démographiques, Institut National d'Étude du Travail et d'Orientation Professionnelle, *Enquête nationale sur le niveau intellectuel des enfants d'âge scolaire*, Paris, Presses Universitaires de France, 1969.

In regard to differences according to sex, the main findings were, first, that the proportion of repeaters in the final grade of primary education was the same for both boys and girls; and, second, that the admission rate to the first year of secondary education (*classe de 6e*)[1] was around 55%, with little difference between the sexes. 'Girls however were slightly ahead of boys ... on the other hand there were slightly more boys than girls in the lycées and slightly fewer in the CEGs[2] (27% boys as against 26% girls in the lycées, 27% and 29% respectively in the CEGs'; the variations by sex and social background are set forth in Table 16.

The following points emerge from the study on the intellectual level of school-age children: both sexes achieve very similar results (intelligence quotient and graded text scores); the gap is very narrow at every age and in each occupational category; boys are very slightly behind in the early years of schooling but the gap gradually closes and disappears after the age of 10.

All OECD countries display similar findings. The most recent research has been concentrating on the differences in performance related to social background, which is a major source of variation, and in some cases on the size of the child's family and his or her rank among the brothers and sisters, but no variations due to sex have been observed.

One variable receiving more and more attention when analysing differences in performance at school is the child's geographical background: differences in performance might correlate with the location of the place and school. This is an area for investigation.

Even if changing mental attitudes justify a relatively optimistic long-term view, there is still a great deal of uncertainty over the future prospects of schooling for girls in almost three-quarters of the world. Education for girls might well elicit more declarations of intent, theses and ideological campaigns than patient efforts to make progress by dismantling the mechanisms which at present obscure our knowledge of the real situation and by suggesting fresh ways and means of comparing male and female pupils. At the end of Part One, which looked at future prospects, we mentioned the bleak forecasts of statisticians and demographers that the world total of non-enrolled girls would grow. Even if wastage decreases in percentage terms, the very expansion of educational provision could, if it involves rejecting girls at an early stage of their education, help sustain male/female disparities in schooling.

---

1. First year of second level of education.
2. The CEG (general secondary school) provides a short course of general education (i.e. lower secondary education) whereas the lycée covers the full secondary course.

## THE PARTICULAR FORMS OF WASTAGE AMONG GIRLS

Girls do not always drop out at the end of primary education; some of them opt—without our knowing very well the conditions governing their choice (family wishes, personal decision, constraint and so forth)—for streams involving preparation for working life. In most countries technical and vocational education is of fairly recent origin and sprang from an often stormy interaction between production and employment structures and the structures of post-primary education. Wedged between universal basic education and a prestige-laden higher education reserved for an 'élite', secondary schools have doubtless been subjected to the largest number of reforms in regard to content and structure, the most recent trend being to keep on postponing the moment when the various educational streams go their separate ways, either because of the wish to raise the level of instruction considered as the strict minimum for coping with rapid changes in living conditions or because it is desired to imitate more privileged countries. Accordingly, 'technical and vocational education' may, depending on the circumstances, start immediately after primary education, during lower secondary education, at the end of lower secondary education or after the post-compulsory period, or even at university level. Its characteristic feature is that, for the first time in the educational continuum, it offers frankly masculine and feminine—and hence discriminatory—courses of training. These courses are closely subordinated to the kind of jobs carried out by men and women in each society and thus reproduce the traditional pattern of the division of labour between the two sexes. It is not our purpose to examine the various aspects of this problem, whose facets are in any case changing all the time; in every country, non-discrimination on grounds of sex is generally tending to prevail, in legal texts if not in actual practice. In our view, however, it is necessary to stress that one particular form of wastage among girls derives from the fact that they are cut off from educational streams leading to jobs suitable for either sex and are confined to courses of training that make it impossible for them to return to general studies even if they want to.

A great deal of research has drawn attention to the 'guidance' trap in technical education. Such guidance, which depends on existing training possibilities and is sometimes backed by legal measures to prevent teenagers of one sex or the other from gaining admission, is aggravated by the spontaneous refusal of boys to consider occupations traditionally reserved for women.

Even in general secondary education, and especially at the

61

university level, the way boys and girls are steered towards the wide range of available options — literary, scientific, technological etc. — represents a clear case, if not of actual wastage, at least of education that is differentiated according to sex. It is particularly significant to note how the majority of trainee primary teachers in a good many countries, especially in Latin America, are women. Several research projects in OECD member countries are investigating the various parameters which affect the decision to leave school at the end of compulsory education. In a country like France and at this point in their education, proportionally more girls appear to participate in the higher levels of education and distinctly fewer leave school without a qualification, whether in general or in technical education (only 39.1% of girls have not reached the level of the final lower secondary class, as against 51% of boys).[1]

In countries with very high enrolment as well as in developing countries, the repetition of courses often puts an end to the chances of effective 'guidance' which frequently depend on age. This shows that there exists an important interaction between the primary level and subsequent studies.

These differences in the schooling of boys and girls do not concern wastage in the strict sense, but it is difficult to remain silent about their repercussions even when pupils do not actually drop out. Backwardness cannot be regarded as determining the kind of post-primary course adopted by girls, but it is certainly one of many factors that help account for the observed pattern of behaviour. It would be a good idea to analyse the various ways in which both boys and girls pursue their studies at the second and third levels of education by looking into the range of options open to them and how much freedom of choice they are offered.

1. J. Rousselet et al., 'L'entrée des jeunes dans la vie active: la génération 1955', *Les jeunes et l'emploi*, Paris, Presses Universitaires de France, 1975 (Cahiers du Centre d'Études de l'Emploi, 7).

TABLE. 8. Progression of enrolment in primary education by year of study in the regions of the world with lowest enrolment: apparent cohorts (G = girls; B = boys)

| | | Percentage of 1970 first-year pupils reaching: | | | | |
|---|---|---|---|---|---|---|
| | | 1st year | 2nd year | 3rd year | 4th year | 5th year |
| Eastern Africa | G | 100 | 80 | 72 | 67 | 54 |
| | B | 100 | 80 | 74 | 66 | 56 |
| Middle Africa | G | 100 | 67 | 58 | 45 | 39 |
| | B | 100 | 71 | 64 | 53 | 49 |
| Northern Africa | G | 100 | 94 | 92 | 94 | 83 |
| | B | 100 | 95 | 94 | 98 | 89 |
| Western Africa | G | 100 | 83 | 79 | 69 | 61 |
| | B | 100 | 82 | 76 | 67 | 62 |
| Caribbean | G | 100 | 66 | 61 | 58 | 52 |
| | B | 100 | 61 | 53 | 50 | 44 |
| Middle America | G | 100 | 72 | 63 | 54 | 45 |
| | B | 100 | 68 | 61 | 54 | 47 |
| Temperate | G | 100 | 83 | 78 | 73 | 68 |
| South America | B | 100 | 82 | 75 | 70 | 63 |
| Tropical | G | 100 | 59 | 49 | 41 | 36 |
| South America | B | 100 | 59 | 45 | 40 | 36 |
| Eastern | G | 100 | 83 | 75 | 64 | 49 |
| South Asia | B | 100 | 83 | 76 | 65 | 52 |
| Middle | G | 100 | 62 | 50 | 41 | 31 |
| South Asia | B | 100 | 65 | 55 | 49 | 39 |
| Western | G | 100 | 88 | 83 | 78 | 72 |
| South Asia | B | 100 | 88 | 85 | 83 | 77 |

*Source:* Unesco Office of Statistics, *Etude comparative de la scolarisation des filles et des garçons: une analyse statistique 1965 1975* (to be published in the series 'Enquêtes et recherches statistiques: travaux en cours').

63

TABLE 9. Comparative evolution of total and of female pupil numbers in certain African states (T = total; F = females)

| State and period under review | | Year A | Year A + 1 | Year A + 2 | Year A + 3 | Year A + 4 | Year A + 5 |
|---|---|---|---|---|---|---|---|
| Benin | | | | | | | |
| 1965/66–1970/71 | T | 1 000 | 699 | 636 | 577 | 552 | 632 |
| | F | 1 000 | 651 | 699 | 543 | 505 | 555 |
| Central African Empire | | | | | | | |
| 1962/63–1967/68 | T | 1 000 | 629 | 511 | 398 | 391 | 368 |
| | F | 1 000 | 533 | 378 | 300 | 297 | 229 |
| Chad | | | | | | | |
| 1966/67–1971/72 | T | 1 000 | 471 | 345 | 231 | 217 | 292 |
| | F | 1 000 | ... | 285 | 188 | 179 | 176 |
| Congo | | | | | | | |
| 1964/65–1969/70 | T | 1 000 | 667 | 595 | 509 | 424 | 638 |
| | F | 1 000 | 717 | 594 | 495 | 299 | 592 |
| Gabon | | | | | | | |
| 1967/68–1972/73 | T | 1 000 | 481 | 428 | 355 | 335 | 418 |
| | F | 1 000 | 499 | 387 | 348 | 315 | 336 |
| Ivory Coast | | | | | | | |
| 1966/67–1971/72 | T | 1 000 | 780 | 735 | 659 | 701 | 842 |
| | F | 1 000 | 751 | 694 | 603 | 618 | 624 |
| Mali | | | | | | | |
| 1964/65–1968/69 | T | 1 000 | 871 | 793 | 692 | 666 | ... |
| | F | 1 000 | 882 | 782 | 658 | 584 | ... |
| Mauritania | | | | | | | |
| 1963/64–1968/69 | T | 1 000 | 849 | 767 | 676 | 597 | 775 |
| | F | 1 000 | 838 | 534 | 518 | 497 | 600 |
| Senegal | | | | | | | |
| 1964/65–1969/70 | T | 1 000 | 912 | 835 | 787 | 761 | 937 |
| | F | 1 000 | 934 | 837 | 776 | 735 | 850 |
| Togo | | | | | | | |
| 1968/69–1973/74 | T | 1 000 | 625 | 598 | ... | 516 | 605 |
| | F | 1 000 | 605 | 559 | ... | 455 | 469 |
| United Republic of Cameroon | | | | | | | |
| 1967/68–1972/73 | T | 1 000 | 662 | 563 | 457 | 443 | 493 |
| | F | 1 000 | 667 | 572 | 458 | 432 | 437 |
| Upper Volta | | | | | | | |
| 1964/65–1969/70 | T | 1 000 | 844 | 720 | 635 | 545 | 606 |
| | F | 1 000 | 828 | 695 | 614 | 503 | 540 |

*Source:* Data supplied by the Centre de Recherches de l'Institut d'Études du Développement Économique et Social, University of Paris I, France.

TABLE 10. Distribution of countries according to comparative promotion rates for girls and boys

| Group 1 (higher rate of promotion among girls) | Group 2 (equal rates of promotion) | Group 3 (higher rate of promotion among boys) |
|---|---|---|

*In first year of first level of education*

| Group 1 | Group 2 | Group 3 |
|---|---|---|
| Argentina | Czechoslovakia | Benin |
| Belgium | Morocco | Burma |
| Brazil | | Chad |
| Central African Empire | | Ghana |
| Chile | | Guatemala |
| Colombia | | India |
| Costa Rica | | Iran |
| Cyprus | | Iraq |
| Dominican Republic | | Ivory Coast |
| Ecuador | | Mexico |
| France | | Syrian Arab Republic |
| Greece | | |
| Hungary | | |
| Italy | | |
| Jordan | | |
| Malta | | |
| Netherlands | | |
| Nicaragua | | |
| Oman | | |
| Panama | | |
| Paraguay | | |
| Portugal | | |
| Saudi Arabia | | |
| Thailand | | |
| United Republic of Cameroon | | |

*In fourth year of first level of education*

| Group 1 | Group 2 | Group 3 |
|---|---|---|
| Argentina | Cyprus | Benin |
| Austria | Czechoslovakia | Brazil |
| Belgium | Dominican Republic | Burma |
| Chile | Ecuador | Central African Empire |
| Colombia | Greece | Ghana |
| Costa Rica | Guatemala | India |
| France | Hungary | Iraq |
| Iran | Netherlands | Ivory Coast |
| Italy | | Jordan |
| Malta | | Morocco |
| Mexico | | Oman |
| Nicaragua | | Syrian Arab Republic |
| Panama | | Thailand |
| Paraguay | | United Republic of Cameroon |
| Portugal | | |
| Saudi Arabia | | |

TABLE 11. Secondary education: percentage rates of promotion (P), repetition (R) and drop-out (D), by year of study (T = all pupils; F = female pupils)

| | | Congo 1973/74–1974/75 | | | United Republic of Cameroon (1970/71) | | | Venezuela (1973/74) | | |
|---|---|---|---|---|---|---|---|---|---|---|
| | | P | R | D | P | R | D | P | R | D |
| *Lower stage* | | | | | | | | | | |
| 1st year | T | 75.0 | 17.6 | 7.4 | 79.4 | 8.5 | 12.1 | 72.5 | 13.8 | 13.7 |
| | F | 76.4 | 18.8 | 4.8 | 78.2 | 10.0 | 11.8 | 74.9 | 12.5 | 12.6 |
| 2nd year | T | 75.0 | 17.7 | 7.3 | 83.3 | 7.9 | 8.8 | 84.7 | 12.8 | 2.5 |
| | F | 69.2 | 21.5 | 9.3 | 82.5 | 8.3 | 9.2 | 85.6 | 12.4 | 2.0 |
| 3rd year | T | 80.9 | 19.7 | 0.6 | 82.7 | 11.3 | 6.0 | 83.1 | 17.6 | 0.7 |
| | F | 70.3 | 24.6 | 5.1 | 57.5 | 34.5 | 8.0 | 84.1 | 18.4 | 2.5 |
| 4th year | T | 51.2 | 30.3 | 18.5 | 46.7 | 18.7 | 34.6 | 81.0 | 11.1 | 7.9 |
| | F | 30.6 | 38.7 | 31.7 | 38.9 | 24.6 | 36.5 | 81.6 | 10.4 | 8.0 |
| *Upper stage* | | | | | | | | | | |
| 5th year | T | 94.9 | 15.3 | 10.2 | 74.1 | 12.1 | 13.8 | 17.4 | 5.1 | 77.5 |
| | F | 78.4 | 14.1 | 7.5 | 69.1 | 12.9 | 18.0 | 15.7 | 4.7 | 79.6 |
| 6th year | T | 75.8 | 17.2 | 7 | 66.5 | 23.0 | 10.5 | — | 0.5 | 99.5 |
| | F | 62.4 | 13.8 | 23.8 | 62.8 | 19.1 | 18.1 | — | 0.2 | 99.8 |
| 7th year | T | — | 27.6 | 72.4 | — | 28.1 | 71.9 | | | |
| | F | — | 39.7 | 60.3 | — | 29.3 | 70.7 | | | |

TABLE 12. Number of pupils in final year of primary education for 1,000 first-year enrolments (method of stationary reconstructed cohorts)

| Country | Year | Girls | Boys |
|---|---|---|---|
| *Africa* | | | |
| Algeria | 1963 | 286 | 400 |
| | 1974 | 678 | 757 |
| Benin | 1962 | 588 | 577 |
| | 1973 | 533 | 570 |
| Botswana | 1970 | 505 | 488 |
| | 1971 | 793 | 760 |
| Burundi | 1967 | 130 | 193 |
| | 1969 | 128 | 130 |
| Central African Empire | 1967 | 163 | 179 |
| | 1973 | 286 | 449 |
| Chad | 1974 | 222 | 369 |
| Congo | 1965 | 386 | 472 |
| | 1973 | 573 | 618 |
| Gabon | 1971 | 339 | 424 |
| Ivory Coast | 1967 | 459 | 639 |
| Kenya | 1960 | 689 | 725 |
| | 1972 | 685 | 768 |
| Lesotho | 1972 | 433 | 323 |
| | 1974 | 455 | 322 |
| Madagascar | 1963 | 211 | 294 |
| | 1971 | 201 | 207 |
| Malawi | 1972 | 215 | 323 |
| | 1973 | 269 | 459 |
| Mali | 1966 | 427 | 488 |
| Mauritania | 1966 | 525 | 536 |
| Morocco | 1971 | 630 | 579 |
| Niger | 1964 | 305 | 493 |
| | 1973 | 497 | 553 |
| Rwanda | 1962 | 229 | 331 |
| | 1973 | 330 | 371 |
| Senegal | 1969 | 647 | 708 |
| | 1970 | 631 | 723 |
| Libyan Arab Jamahiriya | 1965 | 242 | 481 |
| | 1973 | 821 | 905 |
| Swaziland | 1968 | 348 | 441 |
| | 1974 | 644 | 593 |
| Togo | 1974 | 528 | 669 |
| Tunisia | 1963 | 263 | 345 |
| United Republic of Cameroon | 1972 | 465 | 520 |

TABLE 12 *(continued)*

| Country | Year | Girls | Boys |
|---|---|---|---|
| United Republic of Tanzania | 1968 | 292 | 350 |
|  | 1970 | 493 | 656 |
| Upper Volta | 1963 | 263 | 345 |
|  | 1973 | 554 | 580 |
| Zaire | 1967 | 380 | 583 |
|  | 1970 | 281 | 424 |
| Zambia | 1968 | 560 | 882 |
|  | 1973 | 643 | 848 |
| *Latin America* |  |  |  |
| Argentina | 1961 | 498 | 412 |
|  | 1970 | 644 | 595 |
| Brazil | 1971 | 262 | 227 |
|  | 1973 | 295 | 222 |
| Chile | 1969 | 577 | 549 |
|  | 1973 | 626 | 609 |
| Colombia | 1960 | 224 | 224 |
|  | 1973 | 396 | 340 |
| Costa Rica | 1960 | 428 | 409 |
|  | 1971 | 750 | 693 |
| Cuba | 1968 | 618 | 445 |
|  | 1971 | 544 | 429 |
| Dominican Republic | 1966 | 341 | 328 |
|  | 1969 | 294 | 242 |
| Ecuador | 1962 | 321 | 346 |
|  | 1972 | 570 | 576 |
| El Salvador | 1973 | 269 | 292 |
| Guatemala | 1961 | 287 | 253 |
|  | 1968 | 287 | 273 |
| Guyana | 1967 | 672 | 663 |
|  | 1972 | 836 | 836 |
| Nicaragua | 1967 | 237 | 205 |
|  | 1972 | 300 | 263 |
| Panama | 1963 | 686 | 653 |
|  | 1973 | 766 | 716 |
| Paraguay | 1963 | 289 | 280 |
| *Asia* |  |  |  |
| Bahrain | 1971 | 715 | 691 |
| Burma | 1970 | 220 | 300 |
|  | 1972 | 281 | 338 |
| Cyprus | 1967 | 934 | 952 |
|  | 1972 | 963 | 971 |
| India | 1963 | 406 | 475 |
|  | 1969 | 342 | 429 |

| | Year | | | | Year | | |
|---|---|---|---|---|---|---|---|
| Iran | 1969 | 677 | 708 | Singapore | 1973 | 933 | 944 |
| Iraq | 1965 | 345 | 609 | Syrian Arab Republic | 1963 | 529 | 736 |
| | 1972 | 606 | 699 | Thailand | 1973 | 691 | 850 |
| Jordan | 1965 | 672 | 817 | | 1974 | 359 | 405 |
| | 1973 | 831 | 867 | | | | |
| Kuwait | 1965 | 919 | 958 | *Europe* | | | |
| | 1973 | 942 | 965 | Greece | 1960 | 924 | 960 |
| Oman | 1973 | 243 | 594 | | 1972 | 932 | 950 |
| Qatar | 1971 | 862 | 827 | Portugal | 1967 | 881 | 848 |
| Republic of Korea | 1963 | 909 | 941 | | | | |
| | 1974 | 938 | 941 | | | | |
| Saudi Arabia | 1970 | 773 | 669 | | | | |
| | 1973 | 840 | 753 | | | | |

*Source:* Unesco Office of Statistics, op. cit.

TABLE 13. Comparison of school life expectancy of girls and boys (years)

| Country | Year | Probable duration of schooling in relation to: | | | |
|---|---|---|---|---|---|
| | | Total population | | School population | |
| | | Girls | Boys | Girls | Boys |
| *Africa* | | | | | |
| Benin | 1965 | 1.5 | 3.3 | 7.5 | 7.3 |
| Botswana | 1974 | 6.5 | 5.7 | 7.6 | 7.6 |
| Central African Empire | 1972 | 3.2 | 6,9 | 5.4 | 6.9 |
| Chad | 1974 | 1.1 | 3.8 | 4.7 | 7.6 |
| Congo | 1973 | 9.6 | 11.0 | 9.6 | 11.0 |
| Egypt | 1972 | 4.8 | 8.2 | 8.4 | 9.5 |
| Gambia | 1971 | 1.2 | 2.9 | 7.9 | 7.5 |
| Ivory Coast | 1969 | 3.5 | 6.9 | 7.6 | 9.2 |
| Lesotho | 1973 | 8.5 | 6.8 | 8.5 | 9.5 |
| Libyan Arab Jamahiriya | 1975 | 9.2 | 10.8 | 9.2 | 10.8 |
| Malawi | 1973 | 3.7 | 6.2 | 9.0 | 9.9 |
| Mali | 1970 | 1.3 | 2.6 | 7.4 | 8.4 |
| Mozambique | 1972 | 2.1 | 3.9 | 6.6 | 6.6 |
| Niger | 1973 | 0.7 | 1.4 | 6.0 | 5.8 |
| Rwanda | 1973 | 3.3 | 4.3 | 5.6 | 6.2 |
| Swaziland | 1974 | 8.5 | 9.3 | 10.1 | 11.2 |
| Togo | 1971 | 3.2 | 7.6 | 7.4 | 8.7 |
| United Republic of Cameroon | 1973 | 6.6 | 9.0 | 8.9 | 10.1 |
| Upper Volta | 1971 | 0.7 | 1.2 | 6.7 | 7.0 |
| Zaire | 1971 | 4.5 | 8.1 | 7.8 | 9.2 |
| *America* | | | | | |
| Argentina | 1970 | 9.8 | 9.6 | 9.8 | 9.7 |
| Colombia | 1965 | 5.5 | 5.5 | 7.8 | 8.2 |
| Costa Rica | 1972 | 9.0 | 9.1 | 9.0 | 9.1 |
| Cuba | 1973 | 9.1 | 9.5 | 9.1 | 9.5 |
| Ecuador | 1973 | 8.4 | 8.7 | 9.9 | 9.7 |
| El Salvador | 1972 | 6.3 | 6.8 | 9.1 | 9.3 |
| Guatemala | 1969 | 3.6 | 4.5 | 7.5 | 8.1 |
| Guyana | 1970 | 9.2 | 9.4 | 9.3 | 9.5 |
| Nicaragua | 1973 | 6.5 | 6.4 | 8.8 | 8.7 |
| Panama | 1973 | 10.6 | 10.7 | 10.9 | 10.7 |
| Peru | 1970 | 8.6 | 10.4 | 10.4 | 11.6 |
| Trinidad and Tobago | 1971 | 10.0 | 10.4 | 10.0 | 10.4 |

TABLE 13 *(continued)*

| Country | Year | Probable duration of in relation to : | | | |
|---|---|---|---|---|---|
| | | Total population | | School population | |
| | | Girls | Boys | Girls | Boys |
| *Asia* | | | | | |
| Burma | 1973 | 4.9 | 5.8 | 7.3 | 8.4 |
| Cyprus | 1974 | 7.4 | 7.7 | 10.8 | 11.1 |
| Indonesia | 1971 | 4.4 | 5.6 | 7.3 | 8.2 |
| Iraq | 1975 | 5.1 | 9.8 | 8.1 | 9.8 |
| Japan | 1972 | 11.1 | 11.1 | 11.1 | 11.1 |
| Philippines | 1965 | 7.6 | 7.6 | 7.6 | 7.6 |
| Saudi Arabia | 1973 | 2.4 | 4.6 | 10.0 | 10.4 |
| Syrian Arab Republic | 1974 | 6.5 | 9.7 | 8.4 | 9.7 |
| Thailand | 1965 | 5.5 | 6.4 | 5.8 | 6.5 |
| Turkey | 1973 | 3.2 | 7.6 | 7.4 | 8.7 |
| *Europe* | | | | | |
| Belgium | 1965 | 10.1 | 10.1 | 10.1 | 10.1 |
| France | 1971 | 11.0 | 10.7 | 11.0 | 10.0 |
| Federal Republic of Germany | 1973 | 12.0 | 12.6 | 12.0 | 12.6 |
| Greece | 1970 | 9.7 | 11.0 | 9.7 | 11.0 |
| Hungary | 1972 | 10.1 | 10.5 | 10.3 | 10.7 |
| Ireland | 1972 | 10.6 | 10.4 | 10.6 | 10.4 |
| Luxembourg | 1973 | 10.5 | 11.2 | 10.6 | 11.3 |
| Malta | 1973 | 9.8 | 10.3 | 10.0 | 10.3 |
| Netherlands | 1973 | 10.9 | 11.4 | 10.9 | 11.8 |
| Poland | 1971 | 11.4 | 11.4 | 11.6 | 11.4 |
| Spain | 1972 | 9.4 | 10.1 | 9.4 | 10.1 |
| Yugoslavia | 1970 | 8.7 | 9.6 | 9.0 | 9.6 |
| *Oceania* | | | | | |
| New Zealand | 1974 | 11.2 | 11.3 | 11.2 | 11.3 |

*Source:* Unesco Office of Statistics, op. cit.

TABLE 14. Comparative duration of schooling for boys and girls in the final grades of primary education, Ivory Coast and Togo, 1970 (percentages)

| Length of school career (years) | Ivory Coast | | Togo | |
|---|---|---|---|---|
| | Boys (n = 48 251) | Girls (n = 18 397) | Boys (n = 16 602) | Girls (n = 5 198) |
| 6 | 28.0 | 25.4 | 16.9 | 14.0 |
| 7 | 39.7 | 38.6 | 33.6 | 30.9 |
| 8 | 24.8 | 27.6 | 29.7 | 32.6 |
| 9 | 6.3 | 7.2 | 13.4 | 16.0 |
| 10 | 1.0 | 1.0 | 5.3 | 5.2 |
| 11 | | | 0.9 | 1.0 |
| | 100.0 | 100.0 | 100.0 | 100.0 |

TABLE 15. Proportion of girls in the 1st, 4th and 7th (final) years of general secondary education in thirteen African states and in Madagascar, 1969/70

| Country | 1st year | 4th year | 7th year |
|---|---|---|---|
| Benin | 34.3 | 28.0 | 21.5 |
| Central African Empire | 17.6 | 12.4 | 11.0 |
| Chad | 10.4 | 5.6 | 8.3 |
| Congo | 36.4 | 21.6 | 12.2 |
| Gabon | 33.1 | 22.6 | 17.2 |
| Ivory Coast | 25.2 | 16.2 | 23.9 |
| Madagascar | 42.0[1] | 41.5[1] | 38.7[1] |
| Mali | 27.6 | 20.1 | 18.3 |
| Mauritania | 13.4 | 9.0 | 13.6 |
| Niger | 23.5[1] | 9.3[1] | 28.6[1] |
| Senegal | 32.4 | 26.5 | 23.1 |
| Togo | 23.3 | 18.5 | 10.5 |
| United Republic of Cameroon | 28.8 | 22.0 | 14.0 |
| Upper Volta | 27.9 | 20.4 | 15.0 |

1. Data for 1969.
*Source:* Institut d'Études du Développement Économique et Social (IEDES), University of Paris I, *Statistiques de l'enseignement du 2e degré dans 14 états africains et malgache 1961–1972*, Paris, 1973.

TABLE 16. Social distribution of pupils by sex in France, 1963

| Father's occupation | Boys | Girls | Boys and girls |
|---|---|---|---|
| Farmer | 64 | 67 | 66 |
| Farm worker | 5 | 5 | 5 |
| Worker | 80 | 78 | 79 |
| Service staff | 10 | 10 | 10 |
| Office worker | 76 | 71 | 74 |
| Middle-level professional staff | 169 | 181 | 174 |
| Employer in industry and trade | 163 | 171 | 166 |
| Professional and higher professional staff | 257 | 265 | 260 |
| Other occupation or occupation unknown | 92 | 78 | 86 |
| No occupation | 84 | 74 | 80 |
| TOTAL | 1 000 | 1 000 | 1 000 |

PART THREE

# THE CAUSES
# OF FEMALE WASTAGE

*The reader might well be surprised by the number of pages devoted to what could strike him as an attempt to measure the quantitative aspects of a widely recognized phenomenon. This is not by chance. It was necessary to draw attention to all the ambiguities which crowd around the term 'wastage'. There is, to start with, a great deal of confusion between two approaches: the attempt to follow—or calculate—the school career of a group of pupils on the one hand and, on the other, the observation of how the rules of an education system are being respected. Differences in individual behaviour are thus mixed with the dysfunctions of the system as a whole. In consequence, studies on the causes of wastage leave something to be desired since the exact purpose of the research is not stated. Admittedly, there may be a complex interaction between the system's standard features and the behaviour patterns of those involved in it, but valid propositions cannot be inferred from our present state of knowledge.*

*As soon as one sets out to complicate the analysis by concentrating on girl pupils and attempting to understand exactly what, 'within the system', affects its female 'component parts', one runs the risk of increasing the difficulties.*

*For all these reasons, but also because the studies on this subject are notoriously inadequate, the statistics unsound and of doubtful reliability and satisfactory methods of approach not yet found, the replies to the Unesco questionnaire contain many general comments and many intuitive and empirical assertions. Yet these must not be disregarded since they may contribute to the development of working hypotheses. The inability to provide an accurate account of the problem of wastage among girls has led investigators to concentrate on the general conditions of their schooling. Put simply, it is possible to distinguish between the school system and its shortcomings on the one hand and, on the other, the school's social environment, whose dominant economic and cultural forces tend to be merely condemned rather than subjected to concrete analysis. People are thus vaguely aware that something is wrong with the education system but confine their attention to the general living conditions which, according to their own ideological loyalties, influence or mould it.*

*We shall now proceed to summarize the replies of Member States which provide significant pointers as regards attitudes towards schooling for girls, before utilizing the reflections arising from our previous analyses and various other available documents to put forward a few hypotheses for testing.*

*Before we begin, however, it should be noted that the replies sent in by countries with high enrolment are more detailed and based on more research than the others; they are also more concerned with social psychology and less passive in their attitude to the system, because they assume that social groups may bend its rules. Many European countries, plus the United States, the USSR, Australia and Japan took part in the survey. In short, the fact that a higher proportion of educationally advanced countries than of other countries responded to the questionnaire might give rise to misleading interpretations. We shall try to allow for this as far as possible.*

*A second point is that most countries lacking an other than intuitive grasp of wastage turn their attention to the problem of inequality of access to education. This raises the question as to whether we should accept the hypothesis that inequality of access influences wastage.*

*In countries with very high enrolment and no discrimination until the end of compulsory schooling, it is the twofold problem concerning the decision to leave school or continue studying at this juncture and the type of course chosen by girls and boys that is raised. As we have already stated, the latter issue is a particular form of sexual differentiation in education rather than a genuine case of wastage.*

ATTEMPTED CLASSIFICATION OF REPLIES
TO THE QUESTIONNAIRE

*The replies to the questionnaire have made it possible to sum up the general situation in Table 17,[1] which sets forth certain features of the education systems concerned: presence or absence of compulsory schooling at a given point in time in the study cycle, free tuition, co-education, extent of educational provision at the second level, attitudes to promotion, recourse to repetition, guidance and so forth.*

*By comparing this information with the data on wastage—not always supplied in the form of quantitative estimates—countries may be grouped into four broad categories:*

*Category A: countries having great difficulty in providing education for school-age children, with serious wastage from the first years of primary schooling and recognizing the acuteness of the problem in regard to girls.*

---

1. Tables referred to in Part Three will be found on pages 105–10.

*Category B: countries with the same difficulties in providing education for all and with unequal conditions of schooling for each sex but in which wastage occurs much closer to the end of the primary cycle and before admission to the second level.*

*Category C: no drop-out to be observed, but much repetition; the problems occur at the end of the lower stage of the second level, when pupils choose their stream or leave school.*

*Category D: both repeaters and drop-outs are relatively few in number and the problem area noted in Category C tends to gravitate from the end of lower secondary education towards the close of the upper cycle and admission to university or other types of post-secondary education and training or at the end of compulsory schooling.*

*Generally speaking, countries without compulsory schooling appear to employ a selective examination implying evaluation of educational attainment, sometimes in conjunction with grade averages. Most countries using these types of selection are usually to be found in categories A and B.*

*In categories C and D, selective examinations are encountered only in certain states of the United States and in Czechoslovakia: on the whole, the usual approach is automatic transfer, an approach which naturally tends to correlate with situations devoid of acute intake problems except for a few cases and at the second level.*

*Two or more repetitions in each level of education constitute a phenomenon usually associated with patterns of schooling in countries in categories A and B. Consistent repetition seems much less common in categories C and D but, when this occurs, it takes place at both the first and second levels.*

*These few remarks should not make us lose sight of the variety of particular situations or the somewhat arbitrary manner in which countries have been classified.*

CHAPTER ONE

# CONDITIONS AFFECTING ENROLMENT FOR ALL PUPILS

The reasons for wastage among girls given by countries answering the questionnaire fall into two broad groups: those accounted for by general conditions of a cultural, economic and social nature, and those more particularly linked to the quality of the education provided. It should be emphasized that respondents pointed out that little or no specific research had been carried out in this field. Their replies, therefore, can be regarded only as a first step towards study of the problem. Stereotyped attitudes survive although the general situation, as we have seen, is clearly in the process of changing despite the slow rate of progress common to every undertaking in the field of education. Thus, the replies reflect currently accepted ideas on the subject, sometimes based on research and sometimes on the opinions of more or less representative community leaders. But it should be borne in mind that the causes put forward rarely make a distinction between girls and boys.

## THE SITUATION IN COUNTRIES WITH THE LOWEST ENROLMENT LEVELS

### Socio-economic and cultural factors

For countries placed in categories A and B (see page 77), i.e. the majority of countries and those most seriously handicapped by an accumulation of factors that hinder equality of access and opportunity from the first level onwards, the most frequently mentioned problem was low family income. This greatly perturbs school attendance for both boys and girls and there can be no doubt that poverty, affecting the state as a whole or certain regions or certain social groups, is the major cause of the absence or inadequacy of schooling for children.

Poverty influences attitudes to the school in several ways. In vast regions of the world child labour is essential to the survival of numerous social groups. A great deal of research by the International Labour Organisation on the 'informal' or 'non-structured' sector has highlighted the role of young people in family businesses: as unpaid helper or apprentice the girl or boy has a specific role depending on the type of activity but, for many countries, we lack information on how many young people contribute in this way to commercial or non-commercial production. Certain studies suggest that the proportion of working children aged 10–14 could, if a count were made, turn out to be high. Other replies mention the additional income brought in by young people who work.

This need for the young to work, even temporarily, sometimes comes on top of a total lack of interest in education, whose usefulness is completely missed. This attitude seems to be at odds with the strong demand for schools that has arisen in most countries of the world in the course of the present century, and particularly since about 1950; none the less it is common to many social classes and goes some way to explaining wastage among pupils. Some people do not hesitate to accuse the system's inefficiency and contend that many families, especially those in rural areas, who were formerly enthusiastic about education, have become sceptical and lost some of their determination to see that schools are established or maintained. In our view, however, only a very small minority at present see things in this way.

Handicaps such as poverty, illiteracy and lack of confidence in the benefits of schooling make it harder to accept the loss of income occasioned or to bear the direct or indirect cost of sending children to school. A great many states remarked on this kind of economic constraint. The pupil's clothing, even when not a uniform, the cost of shoes when there is far to walk, the cost of books, materials and in some cases transportation—all these items represent sacrifices on the part of the family which F. Champion Ward[1] has no hesitation in calling 'heroism'.

The poor health and malnutrition of children, often due to the parents' lack of resources and education, are clearly partly to blame for poor results, whether this means repeating or dropping out, which obviously have a very negative effect on the pupil's performance. It is quite obvious that this issue has not been sufficiently studied but, in certain states, it now appears to be of priority concern.

1. F. Champion Ward, *Introduction to Education and Development*, New York, Praeger, 1974.

Two other factors have a decisive impact on wastage. The first concerns migrations. In many countries, the zones of economic activity are very unevenly spaced with the result that there exist on the one hand seasonal migrations of agricultural-worker families and, on the other, a flight from the land towards the outlying districts of towns and cities. This greatly perturbs the child's schooling and we lack information on the education of children who either change school or temporarily or permanently drop out. What we do know, however, is that they are not isolated cases but identifiable groups that statistical resources do not cover satisfactorily. A few countries refer explicitly to this problem of parents who move house. In Guatemala, for example, 'very large-scale migrations in 1968, affecting 250,000 families from the Altiplano, were noted at the time of the coffee and sugar harvest'.

The second factor is cultural and pedagogical in nature and connected with the quality of the educational provision, treated in the next chapter. This is the language problem. The large number of languages spoken outside the school, or differences between the vocabulary of the disadvantaged classes and that of privileged groups, even when the medium of instruction is the national language, is regarded as a direct cause of wastage.

Lastly, all these disavantages are aggravated by rural isolation or a nomadic way of life. To live deep in the country or as a nomad is to combine the disadvantages of a low level of income, a rigid social organization, a less open-minded attitude towards modern culture, a greater risk of being underfed and more often ill with little medical attention, and of belonging to isolated language and cultural groups.

In nearly all cases girls suffer from the additional handicap of seeing their future linked to a view of life distinct from that of men, the dominant social group.

*Shortcomings of the education system*

A third of the countries taking part in the survey admitted to serious difficulties in providing education for all children even at the primary level alone. Statistical investigations carried out by Unesco reveal, in fact, that the majority of the countries in the world are faced with this problem; the reader may turn back to Table 3, which sets forth enrolment ratios by age-group and by sex for the different regions of the world. But, since Europe provided the highest proportion of countries replying to the questionnaire, the information received gives an over-optimistic picture of the intake capacity of the education systems.

*School zoning.* All countries in categories A and B, without exception, stated that 'school zoning'—to employ a planner's expression—was unsatisfactory. In other words, the network of schools is too sparse to meet needs, and many existing schools, particularly in rural areas, do not cover the full primary cycle. This is brought out by the following quotation, which refers to Latin America:

In this respect, the situation is particularly grave in the country, where the population is too widely dispersed for the necessary educational services to be provided under economically feasible conditions . . . The situation is all the more serious as the Latin American countries, in general, are essentially rural, with the majority of the population dwelling outside the cities and deriving its livelihood from agriculture . . . The fundamental problems of education are thus more serious in the rural areas than in the cities, where most of the country's educational forces are concentrated.[1]

Although attention is often drawn to facts such as these, there exist no studies that cover the problem of wastage in terms of the type of school network available. Are drop-outs and repeaters more numerous in rural or in urban areas? In single-teacher schools? In schools with only one classroom? In public or in private schools? In schools providing only three hours of instruction each day? Or four hours? Or six hours?

*Compulsory schooling.* The majority of states in category A have not introduced compulsory schooling, a fact which certain educators deplore since legal obligation would stimulate the public authorities, local communities and private organizations to allocate more resources to education. A considerable number of replies noted the absence of this constraint as one of the reasons for wastage. It has to be admitted that, without compulsory schooling, school zoning is practically meaningless. In one of his recent works, Jacques Hallak speaks of the vital role of school zoning in 'a geographical levelling-out of the conditions of supply through the creation of equal intake capacities and an equitable distribution of human, material and financial resources over the various areas' and in 'equal social opportunity for, and access to schooling through active measures encouraging children to go to school (e.g. setting up a school-transport service, canteens and boarding establish-

---

1. Carlos Delgado, 'Education Today Blocks Change in Latin America', *Education on the Move*, p. 29–30, Paris, Unesco, 1975.

ments) and opposing segregation of the sort where certain schools are attended by certain groups on a race or creed basis.'

Indeed, the lack of transportation, of teachers and of canteens— in short, the lack of resources to look after the pupils and provide them with decent educational facilities—are mentioned time and time again in the replies to the questionnaire as well as in many documents gathered together by Unesco.

*Unsuitable courses of instruction.* The Sudan pointed out that no suitable education had been developed for a population that is largely rural and nomadic; many respondents to the Unesco survey referred to similar cases of badly adjusted school systems. They regarded the structures, methods and content of education as being out of tune with the local context, a hangover from not-so-distant colonial approaches or the importation of foreign models.

This incongruity, which has been denounced for decades, takes a wide variety of forms, including inappropriate curricula which, often because they have been imitated, imported or decided upon by an élite completely out of touch with the ordinary people, ill prepare pupils to work their way through the educational process and give the advantage to those whose background helps them compensate for the shortcomings of the school. The school courses are also too academic and do not stress the value of practical activities associated with occupations vital to the country's economic life.

The system's poor quality is also to be seen in the complete absence or inadequacy of educational and vocational guidance services. Even when they operate, they are often a prey to the very vices they claim to cure, for their staff is insufficient and under-trained. A certain number of countries complained bitterly of this state of affairs in primary or secondary education or, in many cases, in both at once.

When education is not free and no or not enough provision is made for financial assistance to purchase clothing and textbooks and pay for transportation and boarding facilities, the system—as a number of countries pointed out—ends up in practice by eliminating children from the poorest backgrounds.

Without referring to precise studies, many countries stated that they were short of teachers for all levels of education or that their teachers were undertrained.

---

1. Jacques Hallak, *Planning the Location of Schools: An Instrument of Educational Policy*, p. 13, Paris, Unesco: International Institute for Educational Planning, 1977.

To sum up, there is the feeling that the general conditions governing the 'supply' of education are not being properly met. Human and material resources are lacking in many regions, especially in rural and suburban areas. In some cases the language chosen as the medium of instruction is not the one spoken at home and the school's rules are enforced with little insight. A few replies appeared to deplore both the effect of automatic promotion without the backing of measures to enable pupils to advance at their own pace and repetition that overburdens classrooms. Poor results are unlikely to stimulate the life of the school, which is all too often pervaded by apathy and discouragement.

WASTAGE IN COUNTRIES WITH HIGH ENROLMENT

The sample of sixty-two countries replying to the Secretariat's questionnaire included a high proportion (45%) of states with high enrolment; in other words, it does not, as we have said, truly reflect the world situation. Moreover, the often detailed information they provide shows up the problem of wastage in a special light that is not easy to discern from normally available data.

In countries with high enrolment there is no problem of access, since all children are accepted in primary and secondary schools up to the end of the legally defined period of compulsory schooling. The generalization of education in conjunction with compulsory schooling would thus appear to have considerably reduced what is usually understood by wastage. However, there is a lack of more detailed studies aimed at drawing attention to the more subtle forms of 'unsatisfactory' schooling that statistical macro-analysis is unable to bring to light.

These forms of wastage are backwardness owing to repetition (measured by the number of young people who leave school before reaching the normal level of education for their age), the steering of pupils towards special streams for those having difficulty in keeping up with the established curriculum, and the more or less equitable selection procedures for those going on to higher levels of education. But the replies did not refer to these problems except to say that they could not be differentiated according to sex.

The information received dealt essentially with drop-outs. After compulsory schooling, systems vary as to how far they open their doors. They may offer a more or less broad range of streams, varying in prestige and length. To select the candidates who will continue their studies they employ criteria that may or may not be in tune with the living conditions and cultural, economic and social environment of the young.

All respondents agreed that social origin is an important factor of discrimination, and it should be stressed that, even though its complexity makes this concept difficult to express scientifically, each country felt the pressure that a series of factors related to the individual's environment exerted on his or her future.

The United States drew the profile of the type of pupil 'liable' to drop out. Education specialists assume the existence of a recognizable pattern of behaviour that can be discerned about two years before the individual in question leaves school: significant absenteeism, from twenty to thirty days a year and even more; this poor record of attendance is associated with an evident lack of interest in the school and of motivation for any organized activities. He or she is normally two or three years behind, incapable of choosing personal objectives and envisaging a future occupation, and sometimes displays hostility towards the adult world, the authorities, the community and his or her own family. In most cases, this type of pupil comes from low-income social classes and also has financial reasons for leaving school. But social origin can be correlated with dropping out: those most likely to end up with a deficient education are young Negroes and young persons from Spanish-speaking families. The reply, for instance, took the example of five states (Arizona, California, Colorado, New Mexico and Texas) in which the American Citizens' Rights Commission had found that only six out of ten first-year pupils of Mexican origin would graduate from high school and that only about 60% of these could read satisfactorily.

In all states the parents' educational level was regarded as being closely related to the performance of their children at school.

It is not only their family's poor social status that handicaps young people: the 'regional' variable comes in for just as much criticism as 'occupational category' and all the usual parameters mentioned by sociologists, economists and planners—income level, cultural background, locality, size of family, and so forth.[1] The Belgian reply illustrated several of these phenomena: the young are obliged to look for a job very early if they come from large families, from families in which their parents have been working from an early age and are waiting for their children to contribute, following the death of one of the parents, because of boarding costs,

---

1. On this point see R. Poignant, *Education in the Industrialized Countries*, The Hague, N.V. Martinus Nijhoff, 1973 and Organisation for Economic Co-operation and Development (OECD), *Education, Inequality and Life Chances/L'éducation, les inégalités et les chances dans la vie*, Paris, 1975, 2 vols.

etc. In Sweden, poor attendance is more common in urban than in rural areas. Finland stated that a 1960 study had revealed that the admission criteria for upper secondary education varied according to pupil background and that candidates from rural areas or working class families were required to perform better than those from a more privileged milieu.

Certain countries, including New Zealand, drew attention to a fairly recent development, namely the determination of young people to throw off school and family constraints in order to be free and independent. This links up with the observation that the young person sometimes regards failure at school as one of his most effective means of braving parental authority, reacting against an unstable parental relationship or of coming to terms with the emotional neglect of some parents—in large families for instance—who ar not thee least interested in their children's schooling. The desire to be independent is often connected with the need to earn money and so escape from the economic grip of the family.

Respondents often produced reasons connected with the kind of educational services made available: the general structure of post-compulsory systems, the quality of guidance, course content, teacher training. A noteworthy development in Europe and particularly in France is the evolution of pre-school education. All children of 5 years of age are at school, as well as 85% of 4-year-olds and over 60% of those aged 3 and under. A link has in fact been noticed between pre-school enrolment and the number of repeaters in the first year of primary education: the latter drops considerably as pre-primary facilities spread.

As for the zoning of schools, intake capacity at the upper secondary level has a decisive impact on the continuation of studies. Recourse to selection for post-compulsory education is a matter of political choice, even though the pressure of demand on the part of families influences the decision of the authorities. All countries alluded to the problems raised by restricting the number of places. A related point is that the results obtained in previous years affect the choice of those who are 'rejected'.

It was felt that a wide range of options more in line with the aspirations of youth might encourage them to pursue their education. Similarly, it was considered essential to improve guidance procedures at the end of compulsory schooling in order to prevent young persons from dropping out before completing the chosen cycle. Since, in fact, young persons are no longer compelled to attend school once they have decided to go on to further education (whatever role is played in their decision by family wishes or personal resolve), they may leave school because the course of studies does not match their expectations. It was repeatedly stressed that course content and teaching methods were liable to challenge by the young: if courses were too theoretical or did not prepare for what they felt to be 'life', they became discouraged and tended to drop out, sometimes after several setbacks or repetitions.

At this level it is important for teachers to be trained to spot the student who is ill at ease in the structures available to him. Several aspects have to be taken into consideration: training in social psychology should make it easier for teachers to carry out their work in the school and in the classroom but should also stimulate them to establish contact with the environment of young people, get to know their family situation and appreciate their social and economic background.

Migration raises new problems for countries with high enrolment; for example, children arriving from abroad are handicapped by not knowing the language of instruction. The language problem is in fact partly to blame for wastage, whether in the form of repetition or drop-out, but it is difficult to separate this factor from all the others of an emotional, economic and cultural nature that jeopardize the schooling of migrant children.

# CONDITIONS ASSOCIATED WITH MAXIMUM WASTAGE AMONG GIRLS

In analysing the replies to the questionnaire, we shall continue with the four categories of country, even though attitudes to the problem of girls' schooling by no means always correspond to the statistically observed reality.

## CAUSES OF FEMALE WASTAGE IN COUNTRIES WITH THE LOWEST ENROLMENT LEVELS

A few Latin American countries began by pointing out that wastage was not higher for girls than for boys, and this point is confirmed for all states in that region by the figures presented in Parts One and Two of this study. In this case, why do boys tend to benefit less from the school than girls? Are they perhaps called upon, at a very early age, to perform jobs reserved for male children? It appears, in fact, that although more girls pursue their education, even at the second level, only a small proportion take jobs and, for them, vocational training is almost exclusively focused on the teaching profession.

All the other states agreed that wastage is higher among girls than among boys and that it sometimes reaches alarming proportions. Here again two sets of reasons are given, rarely backed up by proof and actual studies but reflecting deep-seated convictions based on an arrangement of present-day facts that sometimes owes a lot to outdated models. The first has to do with the status and role of women in the various social groups of each country and the second involves the design and organization of the school system.

### Status and role of women

Every society is composed of social strata whose members have, throughout history, been attributed an individual status, this arrangement being regarded as vital to a certain concept of species survival and resulting in separate roles for men and women. Many ethnologists, anthropologists and sociologists have studied the ways in which men and women perform distinct, highly defined and hierarchical tasks in the various communities of the world. Although historical and political evolution, together with the patterns of development of each region, have undermined or modified this division of tasks, they have not brought it to an end: it is more or less implicit in terms such as 'tradition', 'custom', 'the woman's function'. Religion is merely one of the cultural factors that may render the outer limits of the woman's 'role' in a particular group more, or less, flexible.

A great many countries make no distinction between the various possible attitudes to enrolling a girl in school and to her educational career, despite the fact, as we have seen, that these attitudes stem from different approaches. Many people still hesitate to trust the school where girls are concerned and, were we to include the reservations of minority population groups, there would be even more. Certain countries with a low level of school enrolment feel that in many respects schooling is by no means essential for girls, their education being a task for the family or group. In some cases it is even considered 'shameful' to send one's daughter to school. On the other hand, it is sometimes stated that experience of school is needed by boys for their future responsibilities as head of the family, implying that formal education, although recognized as important for the future of the group, should be reserved for a single sex.

This general statement is followed by more detailed remarks that all relate to various aspects of the woman's role:

'At home', the daughter has a certain number of duties that would be impossible to perform if she left the house at regular hours in order to attend school.

Housework is always mentioned as a vital necessity: considerable importance is attached to help with preparing meals and, where necessary, to fetching water and numerous other tasks.

Care of younger children, when the mother is giving birth or away from home working.

Female children also take part in raising food crops or in craftwork.

All these reasons tend to buttress the refusal to send girls to school or to justify their absenteeism. Other aspects of schooling, especially drop-out, can be more satisfactorily explained differently.

Early marriage, for instance, leading to motherhood while the girl is still of school age, provides a good reason for dropping out.

Many young girls jump directly from childhood to the role of wife and the unmarried teenager is a product of schooling. As soon as she reaches puberty, that is, as soon as her potential capacity to 'reproduce' makes its appearance, the young girl finds herself bound to the various demands of the group's survival system. When most members of the group respect the traditional rules, the girls themselves show little interest in attending school since they feel much more secure conforming to tradition. On occasions, even their health, considered more delicate than that of boys, is used as an excuse to protect them from the onslaught of modernity.

These remarks reflect the comments of a few Unesco Member States replying to the questionnaire in an attempt to account for what they regard as an unsatisfactory level of female enrolment. As a matter of fact, no more than about fifteen replies incriminated such obstacles and thus made it possible for us to produce this general picture of a situation that, allowing for national variations in extent and detail, could apply to a much larger group of countries.

## Shortcomings of the school system

The system of education is not really preceived as a potential source of poorer schooling for girls.

One state explained that family reluctance was due to co-education; another pointed to the shortage of girls' schools (evidence that obstacles still exist), stating that it is possible to prolong mixed education in the same school from early childhood and that the conditions for implementing co-education in certain regions should be thoroughly examined. These states regretted both the shortage of female teachers and the fact that they were relatively less qualified than their male colleagues. This reproach concerning the lower level of girls' schools came up quite often.

But the handicaps most frequently encountered by female pupils are a direct result of inadequate geographical coverage:

Not enough places, especially in middle and secondary schools. This raises problems of interpretation: is the network of schools insufficient to cater for everybody or is priority given to boys when the intake capacity is limited?

Rural schools are too far from the home and girls find it more difficult than boys to cope with this situation.

The post-primary schools are located in the towns and do not have enough boarding facilities; this makes it difficult, if not impossible, to provide accommodation for girl pupils.

The cost of education was also blamed, though it was not made clear whether this referred to tuition costs, the cost of clothing and school supplies or to loss of earnings; nor, once again, was it stated whether there was more hesitation over investing in the education of a girl than of a boy.

Lastly, educational guidance is particularly inadequate where girls are concerned.

This brings us to the essential problem of adapting schools to meet the needs of female pupils. It emerges clearly in fact that the school passes on certain types of knowledge and certain values which cause concern because they might well lead adolescent girls astray and not help them to realize their potential or which prove totally irrelevant to their adjustment to their future life.

The authorities are particularly conscious of the lack of communication between the education system and the most apprehensive and economically vulnerable segment of society or those most deliberately hostile to the inevitable changes brought about by education. Although wastage is always referred to in official statements on education in general, it becomes a secondary issue where girls are concerned. Everything takes place as if the important thing were access to education and as if problems related to the educational process should necessarily solve themselves.

FEMALE WASTAGE IN COUNTRIES
WITH HIGH ENROLMENT

A number of countries pointed out that wastage among girls was less than among boys, but their use of the term 'wastage' was often ambiguous. Some, for example, took test results or type of course according to sex or post-compulsory drop-outs into consideration.

The Member States with high enrolment—well represented in the group of countries taking part in the survey, as we have seen—have utilized the findings of the large-scale research programme undertaken by the International Association for the Evaluation of Educational Achievement (IEA) between 1966 and 1973[1] on the results obtained in knowledge tests covering six school subjects and some 250,000 pupils— mostly from educationally advanced countries—representative of several pupil populations at critical stages in their school careers. Belgium and New Zealand in particular

1. See the series of publications by the International Association for the Evaluation of Educational Achievement, published by Almqvist & Wicksell, Stockholm.

drew on it for certain parts of their very detailed explanation of schooling for girls.

Before summarizing this information, it should be noted that all replies contained very explicit references to a certain view of the status of women, with many countries calling attention to ongoing research on male and female stereotypes. But the stereotypes persist none the less and show through a number of replies. There are allusions, for example, to the unequal ambition of girls and boys, the former wanting to go in for so-called feminine or social studies or aiming at lower qualifications than their male fellow-students.

As for the results obtained by girls and boys in three scientific subjects—physics, chemistry and biology—the IEA survey showed that

at the start of schooling the difference between boys and girls is minimal. The gap between the results according to sex grows as they get older (international averages for the divergence between the three population groups worked out at 0.23; 0.46; 0.69). The school and out-of-school environment have thus had a diversifying influence.[1]

Several studies in the United States and Europe have sought to show how the school's course content can strengthen traditional stereotypes of male and female roles. Belgium cites the example of the special interest boys may have in the third-level physics exercises, as mentioned in the official classroom instructions of the primary education curriculum in 1957.

This point is taken up in detail in the document provided by Australia,[2] which refers to a series of studies analysing educational materials in general use and what they contain.[3] On the whole, it seems that they provide children with models against which they can measure their own parents and with types of behaviour to which they may aspire as they grow older. The areas of activity for females were predominantly in the home, whereas males had more to do with the wider community. The characters of each sex in children's readers, for example, present constant traits: girls were 'gentle, timid, conforming, domestic, physically weak, docile, and fearful in stress or danger situation'. Their aspirations were confined to 'a narrow list of traditional female roles including housewife,

1. G. Henry (IEA Researcher at the Laboratoire de Pédagogie Expérimentale, University of Liège), *Revue de la Direction Générale des Études* (Brussels), No. 3, March 1974.
2. *Girls, School and Society; A Report by a Study Group to the Schools Commission*, Canberra, November 1975.
3. Ibid., p. 73.

mother, nurse, air hostess, secretary, salesgirl, teacher, model, librarian'. They tended to have 'low self-esteem' and to be 'dependent on the approval of males'. The masculine models, on the other hand, were invariably 'head of the family, the bread winner and firm decision maker . . . unafraid, competent, active, strong, rational and adventurous. Their occupations were . . . physically demanding or else technical jobs, such as builder, plumber, carpenter and mechanic'.

Generally speaking all the studies referred to found that in young children's readers and story-books male characters appeared from two to four times as frequently as female figures.

Australia also stressed, along with other respondents, the role played by the teaching profession in differential schooling according to sex. The 'Pygmalion effect'[1] is probably the most well-known demonstration of how the opinion of their teachers influences the performance of pupils.

An American study[2] set out to describe what primary teachers expect from a good pupil. The answers suggest that a boy should be active, adventurous, aggressive, energetic, independent and a girl sensitive, calm, poised and co-operative.

Another study[3] on 'models' for the socialization of adolescents reveals that girls form a more negative than positive image of themselves. They see their future in a more limited way than boys and their school results show that they interiorize their sense of sexual inferiority. Even though their verbal intelligence is superior, they see themselves as less academically competent than boys.

The IEA survey regarded co-education as one of the factors likely to reduce sexual differentiation in schools. Its findings revealed that, for the age-group 10-11 years old in all countries covered, the differences in performance between girls and boys were much smaller in co-educational schools, whatever the proportion of such schools in a particular country.

In 1970/71, for example, the country in which co-education had made the least progress was Belgium. There, among children of 10–11, a divergence of around 0.27 was noted in single-sex schools as against 0.22 in co-educational ones; by the age of 14 to 15 years the gaps were 0.76 and 0.18 respectively, and the same phenomenon could be detected at the end of secondary education. Thus, within the social context of the countries surveyed, sexual segregation

1. R. Rosenthal and L. Jacobsen, *Pygmalion in the Classroom*, New York, N.Y., Holt, 1968.
2. M. and D. Sadker, 'Sexism in Schools: An Issue for the 70's', *The Educational Digest*, 1974.
3. D. E. Edgar, 'Adolescent Competence and Sexual Disadvantage', *La Trobe Sociology Papers*, June 1974.

emerged as one of the causes of differences in scholastic performance between boys and girls.

We have seen how the children of ethnic minorities in countries
with high enrolment performed less well at school than the other
pupils. The example of Australia (Table 18) shows, in addition,
that there exists a marked differentiation by sex: the percentage
of girls is always lower than that of boys.

Table 19, too, which also concerns Australia, illustrates the
general point already made that there exists a correlation between
the age of leaving school and social background. After the age of
compulsory schooling, a higher proportion of young persons from
families in the lowest occupational categories leave school and
distinctly more girls than boys. For example, in the 18-year-old
age-group, among the children of unskilled workers, 82% of girls
were not in full-time education as against 57% of boys.

# CHAPTER THREE

# SOME QUESTIONS

The replies to the Unesco questionnaire reflect the same preoccupations as the literature dealing more or less directly with the subject. Since 1945, and especially since 1960, publications on education by specialists in all fields of study has proliferated enormously and a great many disagreements over the role of education in development have come to light. Today the issue of women is beginning to follow a similar pattern and, from the historical point of view, both movements are taking place during a period of revolution that has ceased to be industrial and has become social and technological. 'Both men and women continue to run into extremely ambiguous definitions of the so-called "proper" male or female role.'[1] For the last twenty years an American foundation has been conducting research in various countries of the world on how men and women look upon the role of each sex; in our view, the concepts employed in this work make a useful contribution to this study because they are not unrelated to the attitudes of women towards education:

The *traditional* view of the woman's role is that of the other half, her husband's and children's counterpart. She finds her satisfaction indirectly by aiding their full development . . . Her central trait is that she fulfils her destiny by proxy.

The *liberal* view is that of the woman who decides to seek her own fulfilment . . . Her central trait is her attempt to fulfil her destiny through her own success.[2]

Even though various types of discrimination still hinder the access of women to education, their higher level of instruction has led many of them to think about the future of our society, and there

---

1. Anne Steinmann, 'Vingt ans de recherches sur les roles des sexes', in A. Michel (ed.), *Femmes, sexisme et sociétés*, Paris, Presses Universitaires de France, 1977.
2. Ibid.

exists a growing body of research by both men and women that seeks to analyse and influence policies on education. It is undeniable that all present-day systems of education have been strongly marked, depending on the country and its type of culture, by various shades of the traditional or liberal concept of the woman's role in society. The outcome is sometimes sexual inequality of access to schooling, sometimes a falling female participation in education as the study level rises, and sometimes sexually based differentiation in the chosen field of study at the post-compulsory level as well as in higher education.

Other research has proved that differences in performance at school between boys and girls cannot be put down to sexual differences in aptitude but have social and cultural causes. 'General intelligence tests reveal no difference at all between the sexes'[1]

It emerges clearly to what extent the causes of the wastage we have attempted to measure in Part Two of this study can be determined only in a national context: more research is needed. The fact is, the role of women is not evolving in the same way, at the same pace or to the same extent in each country and, within each country, it reflects national economic and political variables as well as different regions, social strata and minority groups. The pace of change varies so much that many contradictions may be observed: as we have seen, co-education helps reduce difference in performance between boys and girls in countries covered by the IEA survey, but in some other regions it is regarded as one of the reasons for family reluctance to send their daughters to school and keep them there.

French and Swedish investigations into the stereotyped patterns of female activities carried by class readers are backed up by our information from Australia—and by a survey of child characters in the mass media[2]—but when we analyse school textbooks in recently independent countries we discover a much more spectacular contrast between the child/parent relations implicitly suggested and the child's actual home environment.

The result is that teenage schoolgirls in many developing countries feel distinctly ill at ease and unsure of what their new role might be. The majority of official texts and statements advocating education's contribution to development give no thought to girls and some important research studies on the development of education do not mention women at all. It might be thought that

1. René Zazzo, 'Quelques constats sur la psychologie différentielle des sexes', in Evelyne Sullero (ed.), *Le fait féminin: qu'est-ce qu'une femme?*, Paris, Fayard, 1978.
2. M. J. Chombart de Lauwe, *Un monde autre: l'enfance; de ses représentations à son mythe*, Paris, Payot, 1971.

they are omitted on the assumption of sexual equality but all the evidence suggests that at the present time female pupils are not taught to be women in the same way as males are taught to be men. In such circumstances, it is hardly surprising that, in many regions of the world, girls have great difficulty in deciding what and how long to study.

A number of surveys aimed at girls in Maghreb, African or Latin American countries have shown that the principal motivation for continuing with their education was, and still is, the opportunity it provided to have some say in the more or less imposed choice of a husband. In Africa, it is now recognized by many rural as well as urban families that studies justify a higher marriage settlement.

In Latin America, teacher training colleges for middle-class girls are the favourite place for passing the time until marriageable age. This explains why the number of qualified graduates from these colleges often bears no relation to the number of qualified female teachers: the completion of a 'teacher training' course does not, in this case, mean that the girl has to work as a teacher.

Hence the marked change, noted quite recently, in the stated goals of education. A humanistic and pilosophical phase, which proclaimed its goal as access to the highest cultural values, was first succeeded by a sociological phase which stressed education's reproductive function in close dependence on the structure of relationships between the classes, and then by a technical phase which tends to regard the school system as having no more than a purely economic function serving the needs of the labour market. This purposely schematic and simplified outline explains why 'employment' and 'education' are today so often mentioned in the same breath, with the former used to justify the latter. Indeed, most published research examines how the various types of education and training relate to employment, how the various types of education and training relate to employment, how young people enter working life, and how vocational preparation and occupation are differentiated according to sex.

In France, for example, many studies[1] have focused on youth and employment, feminine occupations and universities and the labour market, showing how discrimination between boys and girls has been gradually creeping from the post-compulsory level to that of higher education. A survey connected with the entry

1. Particularly the *cahiers* of the Centre d'Études de l'Emploi published by the Presses Universitaires de France, and the Dossiers of the Centre d'Études et de Recherches sur les Qualifications.

into working life of a sample of nearly 2,000 young persons revealed, for example, the following:

Of the generation born in 1955, the girls left school with an educational and vocational attainment that was not only equal but often superior to that of the boys, and yet they are already up against the same kinds of discrimination encountered by women in general.

If we take those who left school between the age of 16 and 19, the girls stayed in education longer: at the age of 19, 37% of girls had left school as against 49.6% of boys.

Working girls had more general education qualifications than boys; 20% had obtained the B.E.P.C. and 7% the Baccalauréat, as against 14% and 1.7% respectively for boys.

It might be thought, as has often been claimed, that girls tend to opt for general courses and fight shy of technical education. But the sample of young school-leavers showed that 64.1% of girls had taken a course of technical training as against 58.2% of boys, and 41.5% of these girls had completed a C.A.P. and B.E.P. compared with 38.8% of boys.

Thus, at the age of 19, the educational and vocational attainment of girls appears to be higher than that of boys.

How do they take practical advantage of this situation?

The fact is, as soon as they have left school, the advantage slips over to the side of boys: at the time of the survey, fewer girls than boys were in employment. From the point of view of the participation rate alone, girls do not succeed in using their education to good effect since they are four times more often inactive than boys. What is more, those who work do so under relatively unfavourable conditions.[1]

These considerations should be qualified to allow for the father's occupational category. For the daughters of skilled, semi-skilled and agricultural workers, it is

as if prolonging education beyond the age of 16 were due less to previous success at school than to the outright refusal to enter the labour market at a particularly unfavourable age, especially where jobs for women are concerned . . . Girls from other social categories find themselves in a rather different situation inasmuch as they are much more unlikely to enter directly into working life.[2]

And yet, it is almost simultaneously asserted that the shortage of jobs for women is due to their lack of qualification. This is in fact true and proves that their present situation, taking into account

1. Irène Kandel, 'Activité/Inactivité des jeunes filles et des jeunes femmes', *L'entrée dans la vie active*, Paris, Presses Universitaires de France, 1977 (Cahiers du Centre d'Études de l'Emploi, 15).

2. Jean Rousselet et al., 'L'entrée des jeunes dans la vie active: la génération 1955', *Les jeunes et l'emploi*, p. 199, Paris, Presses Universitaires de France, 1975 (Cahiers du Centre d'Études de l'Emploi, 7).

their level of training as well as their problems in finding employment, varies very greatly from one industrialized country to another and can hardly be reduced to a single explanatory pattern.

The figures for two French departments show how far leaving school depends on local conditions in regard to education and employment: both departments display similar conditions of enrolment but the local labour market situation affects the leaving rate: at first 12.5% in one department and 10.4% in the other and then, a year later, 7.4% and 3.8% respectively. In the department with more attractive wages, as many girls as boys leave school and take jobs.[1]

On the other hand, a recent joint Unesco/ILO study covering five countries[2] reveals that social and educational investment in favour of boys is still a lot higher than for girls and that there is a long way to go before equal access to education is achieved, except for the first and second levels in Argentina. In Argentina, however, the majority of girls take general courses whose only outlets are jobs with low prestige because the course of studies does not sufficiently reflect the needs of economic and social development.

The point of all these remarks is to show the full complexity of the problem of schooling for girls at the world level. The difficulties of integration into working life arise from a crisis that must not become an excuse for depriving the majority of girls in the world of the same quality of education as boys receive. Here lies the real danger, that the combined effect of demographic and employment problems is today putting a great many women in jeopardy.

A society that provides education for boys only cannot progress as well as one that gives the same opportunity to all its young. The 'added value' which girls derive from education is not confined to the marriage market. The role of women in commercial or non-commercial production is increasingly stressed by economists. Part of the problem is the struggle to have their contribution recognized and made worth while, but it is also necessary to show how much the education and training they ought to receive could increase the value of this production in all areas of working life. The decisive role played by African women in the subsistence economy, trade and craftwork is increasingly emphasized; the problem is how education can help extend the sources of income and improve the quality of life. It is through women, too, that prob-

---

1. Rousselet et al., op. cit., p. 207.
2. Argentina, Ivory Coast, Lebanon, Sierra Leone and Sri Lanka.

lems of health, malnutrition, balance and personal enrichment of young people will be solved.

This raises another point, which joins with the question and cry of warning from many teachers and officials: what education, for whom and for what kind of development?[1] The education systems of African, Latin American and Asian countries are being looked at in a new way:

It is increasingly realized that, in respect of education, continued development along the traditional lines can only spell disaster ... The conscience of the African Nations is also being focused on that sizeable minority (in some countries, majority) who are equally entitled to their share of the nation's resources but who receive no education whatsoever. Certain trends are becoming discernible. Firstly, it is being conceded that notwithstanding the undoubted benefits of education for the enrichment of the individual self, the emphasis in the immediate future must be on evolving a closer relationship between education and the manpower resources required for rapid and sustained development. This means looking again at the aims and objectives of each level of the system to ensure that they are consistent with the society's goals ...

An ideal situation would be to put an embargo on all development of education along existing lines while this reappraisal is under way and to start again on new lines with a new mandate. But, alas, this is unrealistic and impossible. Africa must grapple with the problems of change and development while bowing to the pressures for expansion along old lines.[2]

Another writer looks at Latin America:

On the other hand, as a means of transmitting culture, our educational system as a whole has not escaped the fate of every underdeveloped society which reproduces and reflects foreign culture. We have always had a tendency to imitate foreign models and import methods and doctrines; we are still not capable of working up an educational model which is really our own, based on the observation of our own societies ... Thus a form of education has arisen which is mainly the result of borrowing, and by that very fact 'alienating', a form of education which in many ways turns its back on the real life of the American peoples. In the last analysis, such an education can only encourage the values and behaviour which are compatible with its own proper sense and character ... Far from developing creativity, an education of this type will necessarily be based on memorization and intellectuality; it will assume an academic and bureaucratic form and have no connection with national realities. This is what education in Latin America has been up to now.[3]

1. Jacques Hallak, *A qui profite l'école?* Paris, Presses Universitaires de France, 1974.
2. Arthur T. Porter, 'Adapting Education to African Realities', *Education on the Move*, op. cit., p. 19–20.
3. Delgado, op. cit., p. 30.

What, then, should the system of education do in the face of these attacks from all quarters, and how does the system itself contribute to discrimination against girls? Is it possible, to simplify our grasp of the problems, to allow that the decision to send a daughter to school depends primarily on the society's relationship with the education system but that equal conditions of schooling for boys and girls depend above all on factors connected with the education system itself?

This is what we shall now examine, in hypothetical form rather than as factual assertions, since no studies have been specifically devoted to this issue.

In situations where fewer girls than boys attend school, is it not true that the principles of non-discrimination and equal opportunity favour boys? In other words, are there not in fact critical thresholds of equilibrium beneath which the conditions of educational provision tend to favour the sex that forms the majority?

We have seen how the zoning of schools affects the increase in enrolments. In one of the cases examined, the number of available classrooms varied in the course of a six-year educational cycle from 16,504 for the first year to 6,067 for the sixth while, for a base of 1,000 in the first year, numbers dropped during the same period to 473 boys and 281 girls. But we have no means of knowing whether each class offered the same working conditions to each group of pupils, whether girls or boys.

What impression of the human environment is conveyed by primary teachers, textbooks and educational aids? Are the pupils of each sex introduced to social and home economics, consumption, elementary legal and civic education in different ways?

When demand exceeds the number of places available how is sexual parity achieved? This question deserves further investigation; it is always shirked by planners and especially by those responsible for the zoning of schools, who deal only with cases of reluctance to enrol.

In examining a case-study concerning the zoning of schools in the Daïra de Bouïra in Algeria,[1] which noted low female enrolment at all ages, it emerged that, for the 6–9 and 10–13 age-groups in the commune of Bouïra, more girls than boys had a longer walk to school:

---

1. K. Bensalah, *Le Daïra de Bouïra, Algérie*, Paris, Unesco: IIEP, 1977 (Planning the Location of Schools: Case-study 11). (In French only.)

| Journey time (minutes) | 6–9 age-group | | 10–13 age-group | |
|---|---|---|---|---|
| | Boys | Girls | Boys | Girls |
| 0-5 | 610 | 318 | 481 | 257 |
| 5-10 | 719 | 452 | 888 | 393 |
| 10-15 | 173 | 354 | 225 | 297 |
| 15-20 | 201 | 219 | 155 | 177 |
| 20-25 | 53 | 64 | 54 | 61 |

It may be objected that we do not find the same phenomena in rural communes. It remains however that a certain number of girls make a great effort to reach schools in Bouïra, although it is puzzling why the schools usually happen to be located nearer the boys.

Should we not examine the qualifications of teachers in relation to the composition of classes? In the case just referred to, for example, are there more bilingual primary teachers (Arabic/French) than elsewhere, a possible reason for parents to send their daughters to school? Or more female teachers?

Generally speaking, no studies deal with the conditions of transportation, canteens and boarding facilities in terms of sex.

How can parity be achieved in sitting for examinations? The industrialized countries have taken a big step forward by organizing 'anonymous examinations', and this approach has become widespread. But how are potential candidates selected? Once again, when the number of places is limited, how does this affect the preparation of decisions at lower levels? It is not enough to examine the pass rate by sex; attention must also be given to the problem of improving the likelihood that the two sexes will be equally represented at the next level.

We shall not go once more into the problem of post-primary educational streams with no outlets which, once chosen by girls, have irreversible consequences, since there exist no 'bridges' from one stream to another. Such situations are entirely due to the 'system' and its relationship with a constantly changing environment.

It is assumed in this study that course content and curricula are the same for both sexes, but this has not been proved.

In certain regions co-education has to be introduced in stages since it is worth while only when the number of girls is roughly equal to the number of boys. When this is not so, co-education produces 'minority' situations, a well-known effect when nationality or ethnic origin rather than sex is involved.

Similarly, methods of teaching in public and private institutions should be compared when the results of girls are better in one than in the other so that the relevant variables may be pinpointed.

This list of issues is not exhaustive, but it serves to cast doubt on the contention that the school system is neutral with respect to the education of boys and girls. In Part Four we shall try to examine the impact of institutional measures on schooling for girls.

Before this, however, we must touch upon a particular aspect of present-day education. It is impossible to disregard the changes in social behaviour which are producing a majority of women teachers responsible for education from early childhood to a gradually increasing age, though academic careers still retain enough prestige to attract men. The situation, however, varies considerably from one region of the world to another and we have noted that certain countries feel that girls should be taught by female teachers. In fact, the reasons why women have been and are choosing this profession need to be studied in greater depth. In Latin America the teaching profession has long been dominated by women because, it is claimed, of the very low salaries. In France a similar trend is gaining strength, apparently because the working hours and long holidays make it easier to reconcile employment with family life. But other sectors in Europe, such as medicine, social work and tertiary activities, are attracting more and more women without our being able to advance a similar explanation. In theory, remuneration is the same for men and women, but the educated person's problem of finding a job (for the life of peasant and working-class girls is quite different) seems to follow an occupational pattern that reflects traditional views about the respective roles of men and women.

In reality, it is clear that people in all countries are largely unaware of the historical pressures affecting the problem of access to employment, of the mechanisms underlying the transition from unpaid to paid labour (institutions taking over many of the attentions required by children or the elderly, social measures, appliances to reduce housework, etc.), and of the influence that a high proportion of women exerts on the way a profession is actually exercised.

In particular, has the fact that a great many teachers are women changed teaching approaches and attitudes to pupils? Has it affected the performance of girls, and in what direction? An attempt should be made to examine how women teachers regard the rejection or maintenance of girls in the education system. Clearly all phenomena of this kind change in subtle ways.

The most recent Unesco data on the proportion of women in the teaching profession and the proportion of girls at school show, whatever the level of education, no statistical relation: once again, the school system reacts differentially to its environment.

A great many countries want more female primary teachers but others are beginning to worry lest a high proportion of women should lower the prestige of the teacher's work. There is now the fear that certain careers will be totally forsaken by men, as if equal representation of the sexes in a given occupation were extremely difficult to achieve. A major twentieth-century development has been the entry of women into professions previously reserved for men, but their presence has not yet been fully accepted as the sharing of responsibilities or as a genuine interchange of traditional roles. This is why special attention must be paid to this aspect of the education of boys and girls.

Finally, we cannot overlook the well-known influence of the mother's educational level on her children's success. The less illiterate the mother the more chance her daughter has of going to school. But are such mothers equally ambitious for their sons and their daughters? Further, should not studies be made of the comparative performance of girls and boys where the girls come from a family of brothers and sisters in which either the boys or the girls dominate and according to their particular rank in this group?

By way of conclusion, must we resign ourselves to the admission that the factors determining wastage transcend the framework of the education system? In most countries the history of schools bears out that, once the relations between education and the environment are clarified and once the full set of standards, habits and socio-cultural traditions on which operation of the system is based has been brought out into the open, it is possible to take action to obtain better results.

TABLE 17. Process of education in countries replying to the Unesco questionnaire

| Country | Compulsory schooling | Free education | Co-education | Intake capacity at 2nd level[1] | Diversification | Promotion to next level or repetition | Educational guidance |
|---|---|---|---|---|---|---|---|
| Argentina | I ...6 *** | E | G | E | 7... | C | Yes |
| Australia | I, IIa ...9 *** | E | G | E | 11... | AI → IIa → IIb | Yes |
| Austria | I, IIa ...9 *** | E | G | E | 10... | C, RI1 + IIa1+ | Yes |
| Bahrain | | E | G | | 9... | C, RI1 + IIa1 | Yes |
| Barbados | | E | G | E | 10... | C, RI1, II1 | Yes |
| Belgium | I, IIa ...8 *** | E | G | EI, II | 7... | C | Yes |
| Benin | | EI | G | PIIa, IIb | IIa... | C, RI1+, IIa1, IIb1 | Yes |
| Bolivia | I, IIa ...6 *** | E | G | P | 9... | C, R, 1+ | Yes |
| Bulgaria | I, IIa, III ...9 *** | E | G | EI, II | 8... | R.1+ | Yes |
| Byelorussian Soviet Socialist Republic | Replied that both sexes enjoy equal educational opportunity, but did not supply details | | | | | | |
| Central African Empire | | E | G | PIIa, EIIb | 7... | C, RI1+, III1+ | Yes |
| Chad | | E | G | PIIa, EIIb | 7... | C, RI1+, IIa1, IIb1 | Yes |
| Chile | I ...6 *** | E | G | | 9... | RI1+, II1 | Yes |
| Costa Rica | I, IIa ...9 ** | E | G | E | 10... | C | Yes |
| Cyprus | I ...6 *** | EI, IIa | G | EI, II | 10... | AIIa → IIb | Yes |
| Czechoslovakia | I, IIa ...10 *** | E | G | E | 8... | AIIa → IIb, R.1 | Yes |
| Denmark | I, IIa ...7 *** | EI, IIa, IIb | G | EI, II | 10... | IA | |
| Dominican Republic | I ...6 *** | E | G | E | 11... | C, RI1+ | Yes |

TABLE 17 (continued)

| Country | Compulsory schooling | Free education | Co-education | Intake capacity at 2nd level[1] | Diversification | Promotion to next level or repetition | Educational guidance |
|---|---|---|---|---|---|---|---|
| Finland | I, IIa ...9 *** | EI, IIa | G | EI, EIIa, PIIb | 10 | AI → IIa | Yes |
| France | I, IIa, IIb ...10 *** | EI, IIa, IIb | G | EI, II | 9... | PAI → IIa | Yes |
| Gabon | I, IIa ...10 *** | EI, IIa, IIb | G | E | 7... | C, RII+, III+ | Yes |
| German Democratic Republic | I, IIa, IIb ...11 *** | E | G | E | 11... | P, AI → IIa | Yes |
| Germany, Federal Republic of | I, IIa ...9 *** | E | G | E | 11... | C, RII+, IIa1, IIb1 | Yes |
| Ghana | I, IIa, IIb ...10 *** | E | G | E | 11... | AI → IIa | |
| Greece | I, IIa ...9 ** | E | I, II | E | 9... | AI → IIa R+ | |
| Guatemala | I, IIa ...8 *** | E | G | PII | 10... | C | |
| Iran | I, IIa ...8 *** | E | I, IIa | E | 6... | C, RII+, IIa1, IIb1 | Yes |
| Iraq | I ...6 * | E | EI | E | 10... | RII+, IIa1+, IIb1+ | |
| Israel | I, IIa, IIb ...10 *** | EI, IIa | G | E | 9... | AI→IIa, R.II+, II1 or 1+ | Yes |
| Ivory Coast | I, IIa ...8 * | E | G | P | 7... | C | Yes |
| Japan | I, IIa ...9 *** | EI, IIa | G | E | 10... | AI → IIa | Yes |
| Jordan | I, IIa ...9 ** | E | I, IIa | E | 9... | C, RII+, IIa1+, IIb1 | |
| Kuwait | I, IIa ...8 ** | E | G | E | 9... | C, RII+, III+ | |
| Lebanon | | E | I | P | 6... | C, RII+, III+ | |
| Malta | I, IIa, IIb ...10 *** | EI, II | G | E | 10... | | Yes |
| Mauritania | I ...6 ** | EI | G | EIIa | | | |
| Mexico | I, IIa ...8 *** | EII | I | | 10... | C, RII, IIa1, IIb1 / C | Yes |

106

| | | | | | | | |
|---|---|---|---|---|---|---|---|
| Morocco | I, IIa ...6 ** | E | G | E | 9... | C, RI1, III1+ | Yes |
| Nepal | | EI | G | P | | R1+ | Yes |
| Netherlands | I, IIa ...9 *** | EI, IIa | G | E | 8... | CI → IIa | Yes |
| New Zealand | I, IIa ...9 *** | E | G | E | 9... | AI → IIa → IIb | Yes |
| Norway | I, IIa, IIb ...10 *** | EI, IIa | G | E | 8... | CI → IIa, AIIa → IIb | Yes |
| Pakistan | | E | I | E | 9... | C | Yes |
| Peru | I, IIa ...9 *** | EI, II | G | P | 10... | AI → IIa → IIb | Yes |
| Philippines | I ...6 *** | EI, II | G | P | 7... | CI → IIa | Yes |
| Poland | Replied that both sexes enjoy equal educational opportunity, but did not supply details | | | | | | |
| Portugal | I, IIa ...8 *** | EI, IIa | G | E | 10... | R1+ | Yes |
| Qatar | | E | | E | | C | |
| Spain | I, IIa ...8 ** | EI, IIa, IIb | G | EI, II | 9... | PAI → IIa | Yes |
| Sri Lanka | I, IIa ...8 *** | E | G | E | 9... | AI → IIa R.1 | Yes |
| Sudan | | E | | E | 10... | C, RI1, IIa1, IIb1+ | |
| Sweden | I, IIa ...9 *** | E | G | EI, IIa | 10... | AI → IIa → IIb R1 | Yes |
| Syrian Arab Republic | I ...6 * | E | I, IIa | E | 9... | C, RI1+, III | |
| Tunisia | | E | G | E | 7... | C, RI1+, III1+ | Yes |
| Union of Soviet Socialist Republics | Replied that both sexes enjoy equal educational opportunity, but did not supply details | | | | | | |
| United Republic of Cameroon | | E | G | E | 7... | C, RI1, III | Yes |
| United Republic of Tanzania | I ...7 * | E | G | P | | C, RI1, IIa1 | Yes |
| United States of America | I, IIa, IIb ...10 *** | EI, II | G | E | | R1 or 1+ | Yes |
| Uruguay | I, IIa ...9 *** | E | G | E | 10... | C, RI1+ | Yes |

TABLE 17 (continued)

| Country | Compulsory schooling | Free education | Co-education | Intake capacity at 2nd level[1] | Diversification | Promotion to next level or repetition | Educational guidance |
|---|---|---|---|---|---|---|---|
| Venezuela | I, IIa ...8 *** | E | G | E | 8... | C | Yes |
| Yemen | | E | G | P | | C, RII+, III1+ | |
| Zambia | | E | G | P | 8... | C, RII+, III1+ | Yes |

*Key*

I = First level or primary education
II = Second level or secondary education
IIa = First stage of second level or lower secondary education
IIa... = From the first stage of second level or lower secondary education
IIb = Second stage of second level or upper secondary education
III = Third level or higher education
E = Entirely
P = Partially
G = General practice or becoming general practice
C = Competitive or non-competitive examination, or council of teachers
R = Repetition
A = Automatic
1 = Once
1+ = Twice or more
...6,...7,...8 = up to sixth, seventh or eighth year of study
6...7...,8... = from sixth, seventh or eighth year of study
* = Recently
** = For the last few years
*** = For a number of years
1. This refers to intake capacity in relation to the number of qualified candidates; where selection is practised, therefore, not all candidates are necessarily qualified.

TABLE 18. Status of 16-year-olds and 18-year-olds by birthplace and sex in schools in Australia (excluding Australian Capital Territory and Northern Territory), 1971 (percentages)

| School status | Country of birth | | | | | | | |
|---|---|---|---|---|---|---|---|---|
| | Australia | | Greece | | Italy | | Yugoslavia | |
| | Boys | Girls | Boys | Girls | Boys | Girls | Boys | Girls |
| *At 16 years old* | | | | | | | | |
| At school | 53 | 49 | 40 | 32 | 39 | 34 | 37 | 34 |
| Full-time post-school education | 21 | 16 | 24 | 15 | 31 | 13 | 17 | 8 |
| Not in education | 26 | 35 | 37 | 54 | 31 | 54 | 48 | 59 |
| *At 18 years old* | | | | | | | | |
| At school | 7 | 4 | 16 | 8 | 8 | 7 | 6 | 3 |
| Full-time post-school education | 38 | 25 | 23 | 16 | 36 | 18 | 28 | 6 |
| Not in education | 55 | 71 | 63 | 77 | 57 | 77 | 66 | 91 |

*Source:* Australian Bureau of Statistics.

TABLE 19. Educational participation of 16- 17- and 18-year-old males and females by level of father's occupation, Australia, 1971 (percentages)

| Professional category of father | Pupil's age | At school | | | Post-school education | | | Other than full-time education | | |
|---|---|---|---|---|---|---|---|---|---|---|
| | | Boys | Girls | Boys and girls | Boys | Girls | Boys and girls | Boys | Girls | Boys and girls |
| Professional and managerial | 16 | 69 | 67 | 68 | 15 | 11 | 13 | 16 | 22 | 19 |
| | 17 | 48 | 39 | 44 | 29 | 21 | 25 | 23 | 40 | 31 |
| | 18 | 14 | 8 | 11 | 50 | 40 | 45 | 36 | 52 | 44 |
| Self-employed | 16 | 56 | 58 | 58 | 14 | 14 | 14 | 30 | 28 | 28 |
| | 17 | 27 | 26 | 26 | 19 | 14 | 17 | 54 | 60 | 57 |
| | 18 | 6 | 7 | 6 | 22 | 19 | 21 | 72 | 74 | 73 |
| Clerical and sales | 16 | 59 | 52 | 55 | 21 | 13 | 17 | 20 | 35 | 28 |
| | 17 | 39 | 29 | 34 | 35 | 18 | 27 | 26 | 53 | 39 |
| | 18 | 9 | 4 | 7 | 47 | 27 | 37 | 44 | 69 | 56 |
| Skilled worker | 16 | 51 | 43 | 46 | 26 | 15 | 20 | 23 | 42 | 34 |
| | 17 | 26 | 18 | 22 | 40 | 16 | 28 | 34 | 65 | 50 |
| | 18 | 7 | 3 | 5 | 53 | 20 | 37 | 40 | 77 | 58 |
| Unskilled worker | 16 | 40 | 34 | 37 | 23 | 12 | 18 | 37 | 54 | 45 |
| | 17 | 19 | 13 | 17 | 33 | 13 | 23 | 48 | 74 | 60 |
| | 18 | 6 | 3 | 4 | 37 | 15 | 26 | 57 | 82 | 70 |

Source: Commonwealth Bureau of Census and Statistics, 1971.

## PART FOUR

# THE STRUGGLE AGAINST FEMALE WASTAGE IN EDUCATION

*In Part Two of this study we saw how, in many regions, educational wastage often diminished and became less acute once it had been condemned by economic analysts and planners. During the Conference of Asian Ministers of Education held in Singapore in 1975, certain states claimed to have solved the 'disturbing problem of wastage'. It is clear, then, that institutional measures can bring about a reduction, and this belief underlay Recommendation No. 66 of the International Conference on Education held in Geneva.[1]*

*When we look at the measures taken or examine the results obtained, it is not always easy to pick out the consequences of just one factor or the reasons for just one of the improvements observed; when the task is to analyse the particular behaviour of a single type of pupil—in this case girls—the obstacles become more subtle. This is why the measures adopted (or in preparation) by all the countries which took part in the survey conducted by the Secretariat and aimed at eradicating or preventing wastage usually concern all pupils regardless of sex rather than girls in particular. Educational wastage, moreover, is an ambiguous concept and takes different forms depending on the country's level of enrolment, with the result that respondents made subtantially different suggestions. Countries with low enrolment tended to speak of action to facilitate the admission of new pupils, whereas those with the highest enrolment would often place more emphasis on ways of retaining pupils in the education system beyond the end of compulsory schooling and on raising the qualification level of school-leavers. As a first step, then, the measures may be distinguished according to their fields of application.*

*When we turn to the problems surrounding the education of girls, a second point emerges. On the one hand, efforts are being made to identify male and female stereotypes and ways of fighting against them; such measures include the revision of curricula and the content of teaching materials, the encouragement of co-education, and teacher training in new pedagogical techniques.*

---

1. The full text of this Recommendation may be consulted in Appendix VIII.

On the other hand, a series of measures to promote the admission of girls into the education system is suggested: more female teachers and more schools for girls, when this facilitates enrolment in primary education; and more varied types of education and training when girls are few in a particular sector.

CHAPTER ONE

# MEASURES ADOPTED OR LIKELY TO BE ADOPTED WITH A VIEW TO REDUCING EDUCATIONAL WASTAGE IN GENERAL

## MEASURES ADOPTED IN COUNTRIES FACED WITH THE GREATEST DIFFICULTIES IN EXPANDING ENROLMENTS

Examination of replies to the questionnaire reveals that many of the states with the greatest difficulty—quantitative and qualitative— in providing education have no set of regulations on compulsory schooling. Whatever the particular shortage which makes them hesitate to adopt a measure they know to be inapplicable in practice throughout the country, it appears that, for pupils already admitted, compulsory schooling naturally reduces drop-out. This widely recognized fact is particularly emphasized by a few countries that want to prolong compulsory schooling in order to reduce drop-out before the level of attainment is high enough to generate favourable individual or collective attitudes to development.

These same countries stress that free education over a certain period of time is an effective solution, with the state covering the direct costs of sending a child to school, materials, the cost of clothing, food (canteens) or health care and a certain sum, in the form of financial assistance, scholarships, loans, etc., to compensate for the family's loss of earnings. This appears to be one of the actions most clearly directed at the struggle against poverty and misery, so often mentioned among the causes of refusal to attend school, poor performance and drop-out. Another series of measures is designed to increase the system's intake capacity. Here two tendencies may be discerned : first to increase the number of schools; and second to rationalize the 'zoning of schools'.

We have seen how each of these courses of action can in certain cases help to reduce wastage; the former calls for the establishment of full-cycle schools to enable pupils to terminate the course of education begun and the latter for a systematic attempt to complete existing facilities and to select locations for schools that will provide the best conditions for an equal 'supply' of education and integrate all the relevant human, geographical, material and financial parameters.

Improvements in the education system's retention rate are also being sought through changes in the teaching structures. For example, a country may redefine the length of each cycle of education, substituting a 6+3+3-year pattern for the previous system of three four-year periods, in the hope that this measure will enable it to retain pupils until at least the fourth year of primary education in order to avoid them relapsing into illiteracy.

These changes sometimes involve setting up 'support structures' aimed at consolidating the pupil's level of attainment:

*The establishment of pre-school education* seeks to ease the transition from life to the school but also to facilitate learning at the primary level. It is being considered in a few countries, and sometimes for rural areas too.

*Specially adapted measures for disadvantaged regions* are also being tried out to provide pupils with better schooling. In some cases this means giving a rural slant to the network of schools and their curricula, in others increasing the number of schools in the neglected frontier zones, or extending facilities by adding secondary schools or developing specific compensatory measures for disadvantaged populations and social groups. Various countries have adopted different measures to fight against repetition and drop-out, from adjusting the school timetable to local needs, to establishing travelling schools for nomadic populations or 'special' schools with flexible structures that can accommodate children of different levels having difficulty with their education.

*Changes in educational practices regarding repetition, promotion and the system of selection for access to another level of instruction.* Guidance is often mentioned but with few details. Some suggestions arising from other research will be put forward later.

At the primary level, the most common approach is to try out automatic promotion as a means of getting teaching methods to adjust to the varying needs of individual children rather than to expect pupils to fit into possibly over-rigid standard requirements.

As for access to the second level of education, this is sometimes based on a single anonymous test or made automatic.

Many countries in Latin America and Asia are concentrating their efforts on improving the number and quality of their guidance services. This enterprise is obviously linked with changes in the conditions governing promotion from one level to the next and in the assessment criteria mentioned above. Very sophisticated techniques may be used for the early detection of children liable to drop out or encounter serious difficulties at school.

116

As a corollary to all these measures, one of the most widely used means of combating wastage is the training and qualification of teachers, administrative staff and guidance officers backed up with attempts to sharpen their awareness of the problem. Primary teachers in the classroom do not always appreciate the extent of wastage, its repercussions on the struggle against the growth of illiteracy or what it costs the nation. Today, a number of countries are combining this new awareness of the problem with improved approaches to teaching and guidance within the framework of a reorganized ministry of education and inspectorate.

To help teachers accomplish this task, but also to avoid tendencies to an exaggerated mobility that would be detrimental to pupil performance, steps are being taken to ease working conditions in disadvantaged regions far from urban centres and the principal lines of communication. There are, for example, programmes under way to provide accommodation in hostels or residences and/or financial assistance. Generally speaking, higher salaries for teachers will undoubtedly restore the frequently tarnished prestige of their profession.

Lastly, one of the actions aimed at furthering equality in the conditions of schooling is the adaptation of curricula to national socioeconomic realities. Many countries, claiming that pupils become apathetic because the world of education is totally divorced from outside life, have made efforts to bring their system more in line with their needs. There are many references to the desire not to cut education off from labour market outlets. This explains new options in the field of vocational training, experimental courses in farming techniques from the sixth year of study onwards, full-scale revision of curricula and the production of new school textbooks for the first ten years of education.

The education systems, realizing that all social classes must understand how to obtain good results in education, are employing all the forms of education they can organize. A certain number of countries are endeavouring, for example, to arouse parental interest in the daily life of the school and the performance of their children, to demand their participation, to develop adult education activities, literacy courses, 'consciousness-raising'—in short, to bring the people as close to education and training as possible.

It has already been pointed out how difficult it is to distinguish, among the measures adopted, the respective importance of those designed to reduce educational wastage and those aimed at quantitative and qualitative improvements in the instruction provided. The purpose of the foregoing list of current actions in various countries is simply to put forward a range of possible solutions and a number of hypotheses on which to base future research.

MEASURES ADOPTED IN COUNTRIES WITH HIGH ENROLMENT

The very nature of educational wastage in these countries gives rise to two types of measure. The first sets out to provide pupils with as much schooling as possible and to keep them in the education system beyond compulsory schooling. Such measures therefore place the emphasis on efforts to modify and diversify education and training courses at each level of instruction. Even though it is still claimed that the ultimate goal of the 'school' is to provide young people with the best possible opportunity for personal development and self-fulfilment and that entry into working life is merely one aspect of their relationship with society, the fact is that this aspect is now regarded as it essential, since it represents the normal process whereby young people accede to personal responsibilities and develop the capacity to assume them in full independence.

The second type of measure is focused on young persons with a poor school record marked, for example, by many repetitions. For them, the measures include special classes, structures to ensure early detection and guidance, new attitudes to teaching, and so forth. Many of these children come from groups at a social and economic disadvantage. This explains why policies aimed at reducing educational wastage often incorporate direct material and financial assistance.

The first category of measures, whose purpose is to avoid dropout, includes the prolongation of compulsory schooling. This approach is fairly typical of all countries with high enrolment, though the education systems vary as to the particular moment chosen for guidance and specialization, which can take place either before or after the end of compulsory schooling.

The next concern is to offer, immediately after compulsory schooling, the courses of training most likely to ensure smooth integration into working life. All countries underlined the complexity of the problem, it being very difficult to obtain a precise idea of future employment opportunities in the labour market. In this connection, a study by the OECD remarks that 'the school is now required to play a supporting role in the preparation for active life, social integration and subsequent educational development, rather than attempting to find a balance and precise adjustments between education and employment'.[1] All states are in

1. Organisation for Economic Co-operation and Development (OECD), *Beyond Compulsory Schooling; Options and Changes in Upper Secondary Education*, p. 5, Paris, 1976.

fact looking for new educational models for recurrent education in the second stage of the second level.

The measures in the second category, which seek to ensure better schooling at the individual level, include the following:

*The extremely rapid development of pre-school education*, which amounts to lengthening the period spent at school; one of its stated functions is to ensure smooth progress through the school without setbacks in the form of repetition and thus avoid the retardation which follows the pupil from level to level and restricts his subsequent choice of career (France gave figures of 100% enrolment at 5 years old, 98% at the age of 4, 86% at 3 and 36% at 2 in 1977).

*Maximum flexibility during compulsory schooling.* Some countries are reorganizing course content in the first year of primary education so as to reduce the danger of creating adjustment problems for children with very different learning paces; the basic skills formerly concentrated into this year are now spread over the first two years of study. A large number of measures to counter the inflexibility of education systems are focused on the second level; they make it easier to transfer from one stream to another, and their purpose is to obtain what Austria called 'a high degree of permeability within the system of education'. These modifications are being accompanied by the growing development of guidance structures and efforts to improve the way they work.

*A more individualized instruction for all pupils who are backward or showing signs of some kind of cultural handicap.* At the primary level this might mean setting up classes for the application of new approaches to teaching. In Belgium, for example, the 'adaptation classes', like New Zealand's 'reading clinics' and 'alternative schools', have been established to help pupils fill in their gaps and then return to normal schooling.

In the United States, a special programme is dealing with drop-out prevention. A large number of experiments in each state are concentrating on the early detection of pupils likely to experience learning problems, particularly the children of ethnic minority families. According to a report on drop-out prevention,[1] it is estimated that drop-out among the target population fell by 45.3% during the first three years of the scheme. This type of evaluation is all too rare.

At the second level, measures to reduce wastage include the organization of 'support teaching'. Both France and Belgium are

1. *Drop-out Prevention; A Special Report by the National Advisory Council on Supplementary Centres and Services*, Washington, George Washington University, National Advisory Council on Supplementary Centres and Services, April 1975.

119

working along these lines. In Belgium, the 1974/1975 Reform of Secondary Education created 'experimental classes' to cater for 'problem children and socio-cultural handicaps that hinder normal progress at school'. Their purpose is to enable young persons to return to the *seconde professionnelle* (fifth-year vocational) or *première rénovée* (renovated sixth year) classes covering the first and second years of upper secondary education and thus avoid a dead-end situation. This reform met such a need that at the start of the following year the experiment was extended to pupils obtaining poor results in the higher classes (i.e. *seconde professionnelle* and *première rénovée*) so that pupils in the fourth year vocational course (*troisième professionnelle*), 'whose demands for vocational qualification are largely determined by the needs of the regional labour market',[1] may reach a higher level and thus improve their chances of quickly finding a job.

Such measures provide an answer to the criticisms of employers, who say that compulsory schooling produces young people with insufficient general education and no sign of vocational preparation or constructive attitudes.[2] They should perhaps also be regarded as a means of responding to the growing number of pupils who reject the school as an institution, finding it too out of touch with their particular problems.

A further measure is the attempt to transform the school through greater parental participation in its running. Active co-operation between parents and teachers might prove the solution to setbacks caused by a certain breakdown in communication between the school and home environments or by the conflict of generations. Austria mentioned efforts in this direction and it is a stated objective of Australia's programme of development, which encourages parents to organize talks, seminars and workshops as well as frequent meetings with teachers.

Similarly, in many countries, educational centres run by teachers are trying to foster more interaction between the school and its social environment and paying serious attention to adult initiatives in the development of curricula for schools.

Lastly, there is a general tendency for countries to extend free education, including the cost of transportation, meals (school canteens and textbooks, to a growing number of pupils regardless of their socio-economic origin (France, Austria, Australia). In addition, special measures, usually in the form of scholarships, provide for children from the most disadvantaged backgrounds.

1. F. Florquin, 'Les classes d'accueil expérimentales', *Revue de la Direction Générale de l' Organisation des Études* (Brussels), No. 1, 1977.
2. According to the Organisation for Economic Co-operation and Development (OECD), *Entry of Young People into Working Life; General Report*, Paris, May 1977.

Besides these 'conventional' approaches, more and more attempts are being made—at the post-compulsory level, of course —to supply an ever-increasing amount of information on all forms of out-of-school education and training or on all opportunities provided by the various arrangements related to lifelong education. Examples include the role of the Office National d'Information sur les Enseignements et les Professions (ONISEP) in France, sandwich courses in the Netherlands, evening courses in Malta and the wide variety of 'non-formal' courses in Austria and New Zealand.

# MEASURES SPECIALLY AIMED AT REDUCING FEMALE WASTAGE IN EDUCATION

The first point is that the special measures to improve schooling for girls can hardly be said to be numerous—but is this really a surprise? We have seen to what extent the multifarious causes of female wastage are approached by intuition rather than precise research and have noted the strong tendency in the most disadvantaged countries to say that there is nothing to be done, that, all other things being equal, boys will always get on better than girls. In some industrialized countries this opinion is widespread too, but the facts are there to disprove certain allegations and a lot of research is now overturning ingrained prejudices.

However, a certain number of surprising ideas are coming to light in countries where these problems are particularly acute. Besides approaches that might be regarded as classic, such as more schools for girls, the building of boarding facilities and girls' hostels, the development of teacher training for girls, facilities for the transport and accommodation of women primary teachers and a broader range of vocational courses, thought-provoking proposals have been made in almost all the countries of Asia.

The search for equity may take the form of inverse discrimination. Free schooling? Yes, but for girls only. Scholarships? Yes, but for girls only. Compulsory schooling? Yes, but once again only for girls. A new line of thought, evidence of a fresh and extremely important awareness, is emerging. It is possible that habits of thought and family decisions cannot be changed without 'shock' decisions of this kind. People are at last beginning to realize that perhaps they ought to begin by asserting their own personalities before attempting to catch up, an impossible task when left to the simple pressure of events.

Other measures should also be mentioned. They are less revolutionary, of course, yet bear witness to the desire to take present-day life-styles into consideration: baby-minding facilities are needed so that very young mothers may return to their studies;

they must be re-admitted after having had to leave too soon; all non-formal possibilities must be made available to them; married women must be allowed to study in secondary-schools, etc.

Official bodies—sometimes of ministerial level—are now responsible for the future status of women. Two legal texts mentioned in the survey are worthy of note. The terms of reference of a Commission on the Status of Women, set up in the Ivory Coast in December 1976, included the examination of difficulties encountered by girls in the field of education and training. In Peru, Article 11 of the General Law on Education was expressly concerned with improving the status of women.

Thus a good many countries—even countries with a very long history of segregation— are bringing out avant-garde measures, but it is hard to judge whether they are destined for oblivion or whether, on the contrary, they foretell profound change. We must undoubtedly be more familiar with specific situations and treat broad proposals with some reserve but also develop research methods so as to avoid hindering this initial clarifiication.

Countries already offering equal conditions of schooling for boys and girls and with many or nearly all children provided with education are necessarily concentrating on measures that will transform the respective roles of the two sexes in society. Ministries, committees and many different associations are working in a wide variety of fields to ensure that girls and boys are introduced to life and educated in the same way, with the same standards and the same rights. Many respondents stressed the importance of current research on the revision of curricula, the production of new textbooks, and on drawing the attention of teachers to their subconscious tendency to treat boys and girls differently.

They want women to be properly informed about their actual situation in present-day society and of the means at their disposal to enable them and their daughters to benefit from the right to equality in education.

In this connection, it is interesting to note some thoughts on the changing Arab world[1] that refer to the growing receptivity to education in general and among girls in particular. The main factors in this evolution are

the re-evaluation of religious concepts, the liberalization of the condition of women, increased awareness of the economic role of girls' education, raising of the marriage age, the progressive disappearance of the patriar-

---

1. Abdullah Abdel Dayem, 'The Changing Arab World', *Education on the Move*, p. 25–7, Paris, Unesco, 1975.

chal family order, and the fact that young girls believe they should be educated in order to marry educated men—who were formerly obliged to marry foreigners . . .

Until recently, many parents regarded education with a good deal of suspicion and scepticism, often seeing in it a break with the traditions of society and a threat to moral and religious values . . . This conception has greatly changed during the last two decades, although there are some areas in which vestiges of it remain . . .

One of the basic factors favouring the development of education in Arab countries is the feeling that it is a major means of social advancement . . . Mention must be made of the progressive reduction of the role of pressure groups, such as religious figures and influential village or town notables . . The expansion of Arab societies, their contact with modern civilization, the spread of culture itself, the emergence of individualism and the growth of large cities have gradually led to the disappearance of the social coercion exerted by certain social groups, whereby individual action was confined to a predetermined framework it was impossible to leave. The result has been a greater number of young people, and particularly girls, enrolled in the various branches of education.

CHAPTER THREE

# THE MEASURES ADOPTED: SCOPE AND FUTURE OUTLOOK

We have already referred to the joint ILO/Unesco study on educational wastage published in 1971, which drew up a much more detailed list of problems than we have been able to do on the basis of replies to a fairly limited survey. But all their 'problems and remedies', which take both education systems and outside factors into consideration, reflect the same broad categories as may be found in the present study.

For the full list of measures designed to reduce wastage in general the reader should consult the working document of the 1970 Conference included in the reference work which reviews nearly all the possible solutions for the various types of situation, though it tends, perhaps, to put more stress on new approaches to teaching than on problems of structure. Nor does it make any allusion to the particular situation of girls.

As regards our own survey, the following points seem important: Many measures entail the allocation of considerable additional resources, in some cases in inverse proportion to a country's possibilities. All respondents spoke of financial difficulties and the shortage of buildings; many countries complained that they did not have 'enough financial resources to satisfy demand' for the construction of new schools and/or the purchase of teaching materials, the training of an increasing number of teachers, the creation of new posts such as guidance officers, and so forth. They are obliged to make choices in regard to resource allocation and then to defend these choices.

Yet the link between the remedies that are proposed and implemented and the reduction of wastage is not self-evident. Only one concrete example came up in the survey—an improved individual performance among children from disadvantaged backgrounds in the United States—but this is only one aspect of wastage. Peru and Sudan questioned the effectiveness of automatic promotion.

There is a flagrant lack of evaluation of the measures adopted.

Admittedly, it is not easy to evaluate results in a field that depends so much on the 'time' variable but there can be no progress without it.

We have already stressed the underlying ambiguity of the term 'educational wastage' and the ensuing confusion due to whether one chooses to examine the evolution of a system or, alternatively, the behaviour of some of the people involved in it. The causes of wastage cannot be identified with reasonable clarity unless attention is concentrated on one of these interpretations and hence on its visible effects. All the evidence suggests that research on the causes of wastage with a view to discovering possible solutions would be made easier if, in the first place, a distinction were drawn between repetition and drop-out during compulsory education—particularly at the first level—and drop-out either at the end of compulsory schooling or during the chosen course of post-compulsory education and, second, if the operation of the system and pupil behaviour were no longer lumped together. This would make it possible to arrange all the replies to the questionnaire as well as remarks based on other research in accordance with the most plausible causal relationships.

The authors of the document mentioned above note that pedagogical research has scarcely concerned itself with the problem of wastage. This is because the research has lacked a clear target; the implicit assumption that it is a matter of teaching methods is hardly self-evident. It is impossible to gauge the amount of repetition and drop-out by employing various possible enrolment ratios that measure the annual growth in pupil numbers. We must be clear about this: one country might have 60% of its 6–11 year population at school, of whom only 25% are girls, and a very low probability—say around 30%—that its pupils will complete primary education, whereas another country with the same enrolment ratio may have 50% female pupils and 80% of all pupils completing their schooling.

In certain countries enrolments have risen sharply whereas in others, for reasons yet to be discovered, they have remained despairingly stable—yet planners know what price they have had to pay for their sometimes successful efforts to organize a coherent network of schools. But teachers and the general public are not well-informed and rarely see the relation between cause and effect.

Even though planning techniques, particularly in regard to the zoning of schools, have enabled certain countries to make considerable progress, this study has repeatedly criticized the inadequacy of statistical information—lack of data, lack of relevant processing or lack of dissemination—as to how girls accede to education and then pursue their schooling. One suggested measure for immediate action is the preparation of a 'school zoning map for girls' that could be superimposed on that for boys; this would pinpoint critical areas for in-depth analysis and make it possible to compare pupil concentrations by sex and the identified populations by criteria related to the education system as well as to the cutural and socio-economic environment.

The educational situation of girls cannot be brought out by a process of deduction. It is not like a photographic negative kept in the bottom of a drawer until election time or the visit of foreign dignitaries; it is a social fact that should be made known, especially when it is unpalatable, since ignorance of the facts greatly handicaps the search for effective solutions. Too many assertions are founded on impressions.

A school zoning map for girls could serve as the basis for inexpensive surveys. It remains to develop an appropriate methodology, which could be outlined at the international level and adjusted to fit each national context.

All the measures listed produce effects which are often makeshift though sometimes long-term, but these effects are weighed up only from an empirical point of view. The assumption that girls suffer more from inequality is gaining admission to school than in their school careers needs to be verified in view of the differences between the social groups to which girls and boys in an unevenly balanced situation belong.

Will countries be forced to choose between extending the customary, essentially masculine type of schooling to neglected regions, and raising the proportion of girls in existing schools? How can the incentives or tests employed by a decision-making body be reconciled with the behaviour patterns of social groups?

The role of the information media is obscure. Their messages appear to be highly sensitive to generally accepted stereotypes but, here again, no scientific observations on countries with persistent discrimination are available. And yet it is easy to imagine the potential role of information in helping families, teachers and the pupils themselves to understand their particular situation, to grasp the changes under way and to overcome hesitations.

Could the example of the socialist countries, which have taken less time than the others to achieve equal participation in education of girls and boys, help explain the comparative school careers and performance of girls and boys?

The history of the education systems in industrialized countries shows that compulsory schooling, free tuition and anonymous examinations have unquestionably helped to reduce discrimination, yet have not managed to prevent girls from losing ground in their utilization of schools, and that they had to wait until the second half of the twentieth century to catch up with boys. We must therefore seek out the reasons for this development elsewhere.

It is generally agreed that inequality of educational opportunity has been reduced in Europe in recent decades, but it is very difficult to gauge the relative importance of population growth rates, the widespread desire for knowledge and the needs of the labour market within a general situation marked by the upheavals of two world wars.

This is why simply to adopt the measures being employed by countries in which educational wastage is more or less the same for girls as for boys will not of itself produce the same results in less favoured regions. It cannot be denied that the scope of the measures usually envisaged might well be limited by the mere fact of a growing birth rate, which can cause appropriations to be earmarked for upholding the current enrolment ratios for boys. A study is needed on the comparison of schooling with unequal access.

To achieve a balanced participation in education of boys and girls and equality during the educational process, it thus appears realistic to uphold the principle of a discrimination in favour of girls and to begin considering how this could be implemented.

At the world level, there is growing recognition that the contents of education should be revised. Would it not be desirable to make sure that notions traditionally associated with the world of men or the world of women but needing to be taught to both girls and boys are systematically included in curricula at all levels of instruction? Each sex has overlapping interests within which knowledge converging on a single theme may be discerned. We can agree, for example, that one of these themes is the child, and that everything to do with his procreation, birth, nutrition, health, games and growing awareness of the outside world is of genuine interest to the young. But they could be aroused by other themes too, such as the struggle against everything that burdens the life of human communities in towns or in the country, in rich or poor areas. In this way the school could become a focal point where the foundations for social change in general and for new male and female roles in particular could be laid.

How should we conclude when so many questions remain? Perhaps by condemning the astonishing silence that greets the person who wants to tackle, at the world level, the question of the girl's place in school. Or by expressing the hope that better data and statistical analyses will enable us to obtain more insight into the comparative situations of the two sexes without our being obliged to deduct one from the general total to find the other. Or by fighting to ensure that research in this field occasions neither scorn nor polemical argument but helps to make all people more aware of the problems encountered by women.

# A P P E N D I X   I

## Q U E S T I O N N A I R E
## C O N C E R N I N G   D R O P - O U T S
## A M O N G
## S C H O O L - A G E   G I R L S

## Purpose of the questionnaire

Considerable progress has been made in recent decades toward ensuring that girls enjoy equality of access to education and the same opportunities as boys in this domain. Yet, inequalities in education remain and one of the major problems is of course to ensure that girls enrol in school. However, even when girls enrol another problem exists in many countries: how to retain them in school up to the same levels as those usually achieved by boys in a particular country? Numerous factors of a social, cultural, or economic nature which result in large drop-out rates among girls and/or encourage them to leave school earlier than is on the whole normal for boys, continue in many countries to prevent girls from benefiting fully from available educational opportunities.

This questionnaire is addressed to the problem of drop-outs among girls which was singled out for attention by the World Conference of the International Women's Year. This problem now requires urgent solutions. The questionnaire is designed to collect information on an international scale which will allow the scope of the problem to be assessed, the major causes involved to be analysed and possible solutions to be identified. An International Report will be drawn up on the basis of the replies received and relevant statistical information already made available to Unesco by Member States. The Report will be distributed to all countries and to concerned individuals and institutions.

## Target group and definitions

The target group: Girls between the ages of 5 or 6 and 17 or 18 who have enrolled in school but who have either dropped out or, have left before completing second level. The target group is therefore composed of two sub-groups which for the purpose of this questionnaire are defined as follows: Girls either (a) enrolled at the first level or first stage of the second level who fail to complete that level or stage, or (b) who having completed that level or stage do not proceed to the next level or stage and have thereby dropped out of the formal educational system prematurely.

Terminology: The terms used in this questionnaire with regard to the different levels within the educational system should be interpreted as follows:

| | |
|---|---|
| 1st level: | Primary education |
| 2nd level: | Secondary education |
| 1st stage, secondary: | Lower secondary education |
| 2nd stage, secondary: | Upper secondary education |
| 3rd level: | University or higher education |

Replies

The respondent is requested to use the space provided in the questionnaire.

Should additional space be necessary please attach sheets indicating the reference number of the question.

The questionnaire is not exhaustive and the respondent should feel free to attach any information in addition to that requested, which is relevant to the subject.

If information on some of the points raised in this questionnaire has been already provided to Unesco, within the framework of its other programmes, new replies are not necessary. The respondent is requested either to attach copies of the previous replies with mention of reference number of the questions or, to indicate the date and reference number of the previous replies and the addressee(s) in the Unesco Secretariat.

Sending of replies

It is requested that two copies of the replies should be submitted not later than 30 November 1977 to:

Division of Equality of Educational Opportunity
    and Special Programmes
Section for Girls and Women
Unesco
7 place de Fontenoy
75700 PARIS
France.

QUESTIONNAIRE

1. Please fill in the following diagram, along the lines of the models provided
   below, of your country's educational system up to the end of second level,
   illustrating:

   (a) the levels and points of transition between them within the system;

   (b) the length of each stage and level and the normal age of students;

   (c) horizontal differentiation between academic and/or general education,
       teacher training, technical and/or vocational education.

| Years of schooling | Normal age |
|---|---|
| 13 | 18 |
| 12 | 17 |
| 11 | 16 |
| 10 | 15 |
| 9 | 14 |
| 8 | 13 |
| 7 | 12 |
| 6 | 11 |
| 5 | 10 |
| 4 | 9 |
| 3 | 8 |
| 2 | 7 |
| 1 | 6 |

Models

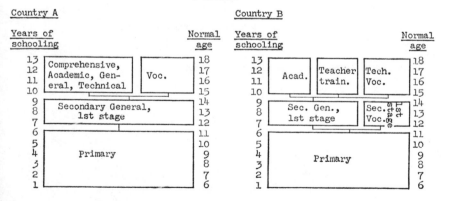

Country A

Country B

133

2.  If education is compulsory at any level in your system:

    2.1  In what year was it introduced?.........................................

    2.2  When did it become effective?...........................................

    2.3  Prescribed age for compulsory education: ..............................

    2.4  Usual year of schooling with which compulsory education ends: ..........

3.  Is public education in your country free in terms of tuition?

| | Yes | No |
|---|---|---|
| at 1st level | ☐ | ☐ |
| at 2nd level, 1st stage | ☐ | ☐ |
| at 2nd level, 2nd stage | ☐ | ☐ |

    3.1  At these levels where education is not free, is there provision for student aid in the form of scholarship and other grants?

            Yes ☐    No ☐

    3.2  If this aid exists, please give the criteria of selection:

        scholastic performance  ☐

        need  ☐

        other  ☐

    3.3  Are the criteria for aid the same for boys and girls:

            Yes ☐    No ☐

    3.4  If No is checked, please elaborate your answer.

4. With reference to the diagram of your educational system, please indicate the criteria for promotion or passage through the points of transition between the various stages in the system.

4.1 Criteria

| | | 1st level to 1st stage secondary | 1st stage secondary to 2nd stage sec. |
|---|---|---|---|
| (1) | Grade averages[1] | ☐ | ☐ |
| (2) | Selective examination which evaluates achievement | ☐ | ☐ |
| (3) | Grade averages + selective examinations | ☐ | ☐ |
| (4) | Automatic | ☐ | ☐ |
| (5) | Other (please specify) | ☐ | ☐ |

4.2 Does your education system have the capacity to offer places to all who have fulfilled the conditions for promotion to the next stage or level?

| | Yes | No |
|---|---|---|
| at 1st stage secondary | ☐ | ☐ |
| at 2nd stage secondary | ☐ | ☐ |

5. At the points in your system where differentiation into academic, general, teacher training, technical and vocational streams or institutions occurs, how are pupils streamed or selected? (Check the appropriate box or boxes)

| Promotion criteria | | 1st level to 1st stage secondary | 1st stage, sec. to 2nd stage secondary | 2nd stage, sec. to 3rd level |
|---|---|---|---|---|
| (a) | Grade averages | ☐ | ☐ | ☐ |
| (b) | Selective examination based on educational achievement | ☐ | ☐ | ☐ |
| (c) | Grade averages + selective examination | ☐ | ☐ | ☐ |
| (d) | Guidance alone | ☐ | ☐ | ☐ |
| (e) | Guidance + grade averages | ☐ | ☐ | ☐ |
| (f) | Guidance + grade averages and selective examination | ☐ | ☐ | ☐ |
| (g) | Guidance + selective examination | ☐ | ☐ | ☐ |
| (h) | Other (please specify) | ☐ | ☐ | ☐ |

(1) Grades are here defined as the notes or marks assigned to pupils' work or performance in courses or other elements which together make up the scholastic programme which rate this work or performance according to a scale of values.

*Appendix I*

6. Is repetition allowed at (check where appropriate):

|  | Once | Twice | More often (give number) |
|---|---|---|---|
| 1st level |  |  |  |
| 1st stage, secondary level |  |  |  |
| 2nd stage, secondary level |  |  |  |

N.B. In case repetition is limited to a number of times by grade, please specify.

7. Please indicate the options chosen by girls and boys at the points of horizontal differentiation within your education system:

|  | 1st stage secondary Girls % | Boys % | 2nd stage secondary Girls % | Boys % |
|---|---|---|---|---|
| Academic or university preparation |  |  |  |  |
| General studies |  |  |  |  |
| Technical and vocational: |  |  |  |  |
|   Industrial |  |  |  |  |
|   Agricultural |  |  |  |  |
|   Commercial |  |  |  |  |
|   Domestic sciences |  |  |  |  |
|   Teacher training |  |  |  |  |
| Other (please specify) |  |  |  |  |
|  | 100% | 100% | 100% | 100% |

8. Is your public education system co-educational at:

| 1st level | Yes ☐ | No ☐ |
|---|---|---|
| 1st stage, secondary level | Yes ☐ | No ☐ |
| 2nd stage, secondary level | Yes ☐ | No ☐ |

9.  If boys and girls are educated in separate institutions:

    9.1 Are the criteria for passage to the next educational level the same?

    |  | Yes | No | Not applicable |
    |---|---|---|---|
    | Between 1st level and 1st stage, secondary | ☐ | ☐ | ☐ |
    | Between 1st stage, secondary and 2nd stage, secondary | ☐ | ☐ | ☐ |

    9.2 Is the curriculum the same?

    |  | Yes | No | Not applicable |
    |---|---|---|---|
    | At 1st level | ☐ | ☐ | ☐ |
    | At 1st stage, secondary level | ☐ | ☐ | ☐ |
    | At 2nd stage, secondary level | ☐ | ☐ | ☐ |

    If there are differences at any level, stage, please specify.

    9.3 If the number of places is not sufficient and therefore selective, examination must be organized on each occasion, please give estimated percentages of total demands among those qualified represented by the respective intake in boys' and girls' schools at the points of level differentiation:

    |  | Girls' schools | Boys' schools |
    |---|---|---|
    | 1st level to 1st stage, secondary | % | % |
    | 1st stage, secondary to 2nd stage, secondary | % | % |
    | 2nd stage, secondary to 3rd level | % | % |

    9.4 Are these separate institutions staffed by:

    |  | Yes | No |
    |---|---|---|
    | Men or women teachers exclusively | ☐ | ☐ |
    | Predominently by men or women teachers | ☐ | ☐ |

10. If No is checked at any level in 9.2 above, are there essential differences characterizing the education of girls in any of the following subjects? Please check and specify.

    |  | 1st level | 1st stage secondary | 2nd stage secondary |
    |---|---|---|---|
    | (1) Language studies | ☐ | ☐ | ☐ |
    | (2) Social studies | ☐ | ☐ | ☐ |
    | (3) Mathematics | ☐ | ☐ | ☐ |
    | (4) Science subject | ☐ | ☐ | ☐ |
    | (5) Practical subjects | ☐ | ☐ | ☐ |
    | (6) Aesthetic subjects | ☐ | ☐ | ☐ |

11. Is educational and vocational guidance included in the educational system of your country?

        Yes ☐         No ☐

In the case of an affirmative reply:

11.1 Is this guidance intended to direct:

    1st level leavers to 1st stage, secondary education ☐

    1st level leavers and drop-outs to work ☐

    1st stage, secondary leavers to 2nd stage, secondary education ☐

    1st stage, secondary leavers and drop-outs to work ☐

    2nd stage, secondary drop-outs to work ☐

    2nd stage, secondary leavers to 3rd level ☐

11.2 Do the same programmes apply to both boys and girls?

        Yes ☐         No ☐

If No is checked, please specify.

11.3 Are special efforts being made to help girls choose their field of studies, to encourage them to pursue their education and to prepare them for professional careers other than the stereotype patterns?

        Yes ☐         No ☐

12. Please identify the reasons which cause children and young people to drop out or leave school early:

| | 1st level | | 1st stage, sec. | | 2nd stage, sec. | |
|---|---|---|---|---|---|---|
| | Boys | Girls | Boys | Girls | Boys | Girls |
| I. Reasons related to the education system | | | | | | |
| A. Problems in overall policy and organization | | | | | | |
| 1. Education not compulsory | ☐ | ☐ | ☐ | ☐ | ☐ | ☐ |
| 2. Co-education not implemented | ☐ | ☐ | ☐ | ☐ | ☐ | ☐ |

| | 1st level | | 1st stage, sec. | | 2nd stage, sec. | |
|---|---|---|---|---|---|---|
| B. Inadequate physical capacity and staff | Boys | Girls | Boys | Girls | Boys | Girls |
| 3. Lack of places in schools existing in communities | ☐ | ☐ | ☐ | ☐ | ☐ | ☐ |
| 4. Lack of schools in communities | ☐ | ☐ | ☐ | ☐ | ☐ | ☐ |
| 5. Lack of boarding facilities when schools distant from communities | ☐ | ☐ | ☐ | ☐ | ☐ | ☐ |
| 6. Lack of transport facilities when schools distant from communities | ☐ | ☐ | ☐ | ☐ | ☐ | ☐ |
| 7. Lack of teachers | | | | | | |
| C. Education is not entirely free | | | | | | |
| 8. Cost of tuition | ☐ | ☐ | ☐ | ☐ | ☐ | ☐ |
| 9. Cost of books and supplies | ☐ | ☐ | ☐ | ☐ | ☐ | ☐ |
| 10. Cost of boarding | ☐ | ☐ | ☐ | ☐ | ☐ | ☐ |
| 11. Cost of transport | ☐ | ☐ | ☐ | ☐ | ☐ | ☐ |
| 12. Inadequate financial aid to pupils | ☐ | ☐ | ☐ | ☐ | ☐ | ☐ |
| D. Quality of education not adequate to meet needs | | | | | | |
| 13. Unqualified teachers | ☐ | ☐ | ☐ | ☐ | ☐ | ☐ |
| 14. Not enough women teachers to act as incentive to female retention in schools | ☐ | ☐ | ☐ | ☐ | ☐ | ☐ |
| 15. Curricula not adapted to local conditions and real learning needs | ☐ | ☐ | ☐ | ☐ | ☐ | ☐ |
| 16. Language used in schools differs from native language | ☐ | ☐ | ☐ | ☐ | ☐ | ☐ |
| 17. Education provided does not adequately prepare pupils for following level and stage | ☐ | ☐ | ☐ | ☐ | ☐ | ☐ |
| 18. Education lacks practical element preparing pupils for world of work | ☐ | ☐ | ☐ | ☐ | ☐ | ☐ |
| 19. Preference for short literacy courses or post-literacy courses in conjunction with practical training or employment | ☐ | ☐ | ☐ | ☐ | ☐ | ☐ |
| 20. Educational guidance lacking or inadequate | ☐ | ☐ | ☐ | ☐ | ☐ | ☐ |
| 21. Vocational guidance lacking or inadequate | ☐ | ☐ | ☐ | ☐ | ☐ | ☐ |

139

| | 1st level | | 1st stage, sec. | | 2nd stage, sec. | |
|---|---|---|---|---|---|---|
| | Boys | Girls | Boys | Girls | Boys | Girls |

**II.** Reasons related to the individual

22. Discouragement because of poor scholastic performance ☐ ☐ ☐ ☐ ☐ ☐

23. Discouragement because of repetition ☐ ☐ ☐ ☐ ☐ ☐

24. Poor health ☐ ☐ ☐ ☐ ☐ ☐

25. Children wish to be independent of family ☐ ☐ ☐ ☐ ☐ ☐

**III.** Reasons related to socio-economic status of family

26. Family income does not permit leaving children to stay in school ☐ ☐ ☐ ☐ ☐ ☐

27. Family socio-economic status such that education not seen necessary to children's future roles ☐ ☐ ☐ ☐ ☐ ☐

28. Frequent change of domicile due to parents' work ☐ ☐ ☐ ☐ ☐ ☐

29. Children needed to help in family's work or profession ☐ ☐ ☐ ☐ ☐ ☐

30. Children needed to help in home because mother works ☐ ☐ ☐ ☐ ☐ ☐

31. Children's income needed to supplement family income ☐ ☐ ☐ ☐ ☐ ☐

**IV.** Reasons related to sociological and cultural patterns

If sociological and cultural factors have a significant impact on drop-outs amongst school-age girls, please specify.

**V.** Other reasons

13. List in <u>order of importance</u> the designated numbers of the causes, identified in 12 above, of drop-outs and early school leavers among girls and boys at each level:

| <u>1st level</u> | | 1st stage,<br><u>secondary</u> | | 2nd stage,<br><u>secondary</u> | |
|---|---|---|---|---|---|
| Girls | Boys | Girls | Boys | Girls | Boys |

14. Taking the causes mentioned in 12 above for <u>girls</u> dropping out or leaving school early, indicate the differences, if any, between urban and rural areas by circling the appropriate number:

| Urban | | | Rural | | |
|---|---|---|---|---|---|
| 1st level | 1st stage, secondary | 2nd stage, secondary | 1st level | 1st stage, secondary | 2nd stage, secondary |
| 1 | 1 | 1 | 1 | 1 | 1 |
| 2 | 2 | 2 | 2 | 2 | 2 |
| 3 | 3 | 3 | 3 | 3 | 3 |
| 4 | 4 | 4 | 4 | 4 | 4 |
| 5 | 5 | 5 | 5 | 5 | 5 |
| 6 | 6 | 6 | 6 | 6 | 6 |
| 7 | 7 | 7 | 7 | 7 | 7 |
| 8 | 8 | 8 | 8 | 8 | 8 |
| 9 | 9 | 9 | 9 | 9 | 9 |
| 10 | 10 | 10 | 10 | 10 | 10 |
| 11 | 11 | 11 | 11 | 11 | 11 |
| 12 | 12 | 12 | 12 | 12 | 12 |
| 13 | 13 | 13 | 13 | 13 | 13 |
| 14 | 14 | 14 | 14 | 14 | 14 |
| 15 | 15 | 15 | 15 | 15 | 15 |
| 16 | 16 | 16 | 16 | 16 | 16 |
| 17 | 17 | 17 | 17 | 17 | 17 |
| 18 | 18 | 18 | 18 | 18 | 18 |
| 19 | 19 | 19 | 19 | 19 | 19 |
| 20 | 20 | 20 | 20 | 20 | 20 |
| 21 | 21 | 21 | 21 | 21 | 21 |
| 22 | 22 | 22 | 22 | 22 | 22 |
| 23 | 23 | 23 | 23 | 23 | 23 |
| 24 | 24 | 24 | 24 | 24 | 24 |
| 25 | 25 | 25 | 25 | 25 | 25 |
| 26 | 26 | 26 | 26 | 26 | 26 |
| 27 | 27 | 27 | 27 | 27 | 27 |
| 28 | 28 | 28 | 28 | 28 | 28 |
| 29 | 29 | 29 | 29 | 29 | 29 |
| 30 | 30 | 30 | 30 | 30 | 30 |
| 31 | 31 | 31 | 31 | 31 | 31 |

15. Using additional sheets, please elaborate on the information provided in 12, 13 and 14 above, analysing the major reasons for dropping out among girls, the differences distinguished between girls and boys and the differences if any between urban and rural areas. In your analysis please discuss any relationships which may exist between reasons within one category (e.g. in Category II poor health may be linked to poor scholastic performance and this in turn linked to repetition) and between categories (e.g. reasons for drop out in categories I.C and II may be linked closely to low family socio-economic status).

16. Please describe as appropriate: (i) your country's experience with regard to policies adopted and measures taken; or (ii) your country's plan to encourage girls to enrol and remain in school. Such measures might be broad (for example, making compulsory education effective, instituting co-education or offering facilities to pre-school children from culturally deprived background which will increase their chances of success in later formal schooling) or they might be directed to eliminating certain specific causes or sets of causes for dropping out and early leaving (for example, establishment of improved teacher-training programmes, curriculum innovation, establishment of boarding schools for girls in rural areas, development of educational and vocational guidance. Relate these policies and measures to the general problems or causes at which they were directed and note the impact or results obtained (please use additional sheets if necessary).

General problem or causes of dropping out or leaving early:

Policies adopted or measures taken or planned:

Results obtained or expected:

Difficulties encountered in implementation and other remarks:

General problem or causes of dropping out or leaving early:

Policies adopted or measures taken or planned:

Results obtained or expected:

Difficulties encountered in implementation and other remarks:

17. If data are available or estimations are possible, please indicate the activities of those girls between the ages of 5 or 6 and 17 or 18 who are outside the school system (girls who have dropped out or left school early), according to the following table:

| Activity | 1st level drop-outs | 1st level leavers | 1st stage, secondary drop-outs | 1st stage, secondary leavers | 2nd stage, secondary drop-outs |
|---|---|---|---|---|---|
| (1) Vocational training | _____% | _____% | _____% | _____% | _____% |
| (2) Employment | _____% | _____% | _____% | _____% | _____% |
| (3) At home | _____% | _____% | _____% | _____% | _____% |
| (4) Vocational training and attendance at literacy, etc. | _____% | _____% | _____% | _____% | _____% |
| (5) Employment and attendance at literacy, etc. | _____% | _____% | _____% | _____% | _____% |
| (6) At home and attendance at literacy, etc. | _____% | _____% | _____% | _____% | _____% |
| (7) Others (please specify) | _____% | _____% | _____% | _____% | _____% |
| (8) Unknown | _____% | _____% | _____% | _____% | _____% |
| | 100% | 100% | 100% | 100% | 100% |

18. What measures are planned or have been taken to offer more educational opportunities to the groups identified in 17 above?

    (1) Development of vocational training programmes:  Urban ☐

                                                           Rural ☐

    (2) Opportunities to re-enter the educational system  ☐

    (3) Correspondence and/or evening classes leading to awards and qualifications equal to those obtained under the regular system ☐

    (4) Literacy programmes ☐

    (5) Post literacy programmes ☐

    (6) Special guidance programmes ☐

    (7) Mass educational programmes ☐

    (8) Other (please specify) ☐

19. Please describe in some detail the more important of the measures indicated
    in 18 above, including provision made to encourage girls to take advantage
    of these opportunities (if necessary, attach an additional sheet).

20. Please elaborate on any of the above questions which are especially relevant to the situation in your country, in order to provide a clear picture of the problems and of the solutions now being worked out, with regard to encouraging girls to take full advantage of the educational opportunities open to them and to creating further opportunities.

21. Please provide a bibliography of the studies and inquiries carried out on the drop-outs and early school leavers among school-age girls and, if possible, provide the Secretariat of Unesco with two copies of each of the most important reports or publications.

# COMPOSITION OF MACRO-REGIONS
## AND COMPONENT REGIONS [1]

AFRICA

*Western Africa*

Benin
Cape Verde
Gambia
Ghana
Guinea
Guinea-Bissau
Ivory Coast
Liberia
Mali
Mauritania
Niger
Nigeria
St. Helena
Senegal
Sierra Leone
Togo
Upper Volta

*Eastern Africa*

British Indian
  Ocean Territory
Burundi
Comoros
Djibouti
Ethiopia
Kenya
Madagascar
Malawi
Mauritius

Mozambique
Réunion
Rwanda
Seychelles
Somalia
Southern Rhodesia
Uganda
United Republic
  of Tanzania
Zambia

*Northern Africa*

Algeria
Egypt
Libyan Arab
  Jamahiriya
Morocco
Sudan
Tunisia
Western Sahara

*Middle Africa*

Angola (including
  Cabinda)
Central African Empire
Chad
Congo
Equatorial Guinea
Gabon
São Tomé and
  Principe

United Republic
  of Cameroon
Zaire

*Southern Africa*

Botswana
Lesotho
Namibia
South Africa
Swaziland

NORTHERN
  AMERICA*

Bermuda
Canada
Greenland
St. Pierre
  and Miquelon
United States
  (including
  Hawaii)

LATIN AMERICA

*Tropical South America*

Bolivia
Brazil
Colombia
Ecuador

1. Regions classified as MDRs (More Developed Regions) are indicated by an asterisk.

French Guiana
Guyana
Paraguay
Peru
Surinam
Venezuela

*Middle America
( Mainland)*

Belize
Canal Zone (Panama)
Costa Rica
El Salvador
Guatemala
Honduras
Mexico
Nicaragua
Panama

*Temperate South America**

Argentina
Chile
Falkland Islands
(Malvinas)
Uruguay

*Caribbean*

Antigua
Bahamas
Barbados
British Virgin Islands
Cayman Islands
Cuba
Dominica
Dominican Republic
Grenada
Guadeloupe
Haiti
Jamaica
Martinique
Montserrat
Netherlands Antilles
Puerto Rico
St. Kitts-Nevis-
Anguilla
St. Lucia
St. Vincent
Trinidad and Tobago

Turks and Caicos
Islands
United States Virgin
Islands

EAST ASIA

*China*

*Japan**

*Other East Asia*

Hong Kong
Korea
Democratic People's
Republic of Korea
Republic of Korea
Macau
Mongolia

SOUTH ASIA

*Middle South Asia*

Afghanistan
Bangladesh
Bhutan
India
Iran
Maldives
Nepal
Pakistan
Sri Lanka

*Eastern South Asia*

Brunei
Burma
Democratic
Kampuchea
East Timor
Indonesia
Lao People's
Democratic
Republic
Malaysia
Philippines
Singapore

Thailand
Viet Nam

*Western South Asia*

Bahrain
Cyprus
Gaza Strip (Palestine)
Iraq
Israel
Jordan
Kuwait
Lebanon
Oman
Qatar
Saudi Arabia
Syrian Arab Republic
Turkey
United Arab Emirates
Yemen
Yemen, Democratic

EUROPE

*Western Europe**

Austria
Belgium
France
Germany, Federal
Republic of
Liechtenstein
Luxembourg
Monaco
Netherlands
Switzerland

*Southern Europe**

Albania
Andorra
Gibraltar
Greece
Holy See
Italy
Malta
Portugal
San Marino

151

*Southorm Europe (continued)*

Spain
Yugoslavia

*Eastern Europe\**

Bulgaria
Czechoslovakia
German Democratic
    Republic
Hungary
Poland
Romania

*Northern Europe\**

Channel Islands
Denmark
Faeroe Islands
Finland
Iceland
Ireland
Isle of Man
Norway
Sweden
United Kingdom

OCEANIA

*Australia and New Zealand\**

Australia
New Zealand

*Melanesia*

New Caledonia
New Hebrides
Norfolk Island
Papua New Guinea
Solomon Islands

*Micronesia-Polynesia*

*Polynesia*

American Samoa
Cook Islands
Fiji
French Polynesia
Tonga
Wallis and Futuna
    Islands

Samoa

*Micronesia*

Canton and Enderbury
    Islands
Christmas Island
Cocos (Keeling)
    Islands
Gilbert Islands
Guam
Johnston Island
Midway Island
Nauru
Niue
Pacific Islands
Pitcairn Island
Tokelau
Tuvalu
Wake Island

UNION OF SOVIET
SOCIALIST
REPUBLICS\*

*Source:* United Nations, Department of International Economic and Social Affairs, *Demographic Yearbook, 1977/Annuaire démographique, 1977,* p. 27, New York, 1978.

# DISTRIBUTION OF DEVELOPING COUNTRIES BY ENROLMENT RATIO OF GIRLS AGED BETWEEN 6 AND 23 YEARS, 1965

| Under 10% (25 countries) | 10–19% (13 countries) | 20–29% (15 countries) |
|---|---|---|
| Afghanistan | Central African Empire | Algeria |
| Angola | Haiti | Bolivia |
| Bangladesh | Ivory Coast | Egypt |
| Benin | Kenya | Equatorial Guinea |
| Bhutan | Libyan Arab Jamahiriya | Guatemala |
| Burundi | Malawi | India |
| Chad | Morocco | Indonesia |
| Democratic Yemen | Nigeria | Iran |
| Ethiopia | Senegal | Iraq |
| Gambia | Sierra Leone | Madagascar |
| Guinea | Togo | Rwanda |
| Guinea-Bissau | United Republic of Tanzania | Syrian Arab Republic |
| Liberia | Zaire | Uganda |
| Mali | | United Republic of Cameroon |
| Mauritania | | Zambia |
| Mozambique | | |
| Nepal | | |
| Niger | | |
| Oman | | |
| Pakistan | | |
| Saudi Arabia | | |
| Somalia | | |
| Sudan | | |
| Upper Volta | | |
| Yemen | | |

*Source:* Unesco Office of Statistics, *Étude comparative de la scolarisation des filles et des garçons: une analyse statistique 1965–1975* (to be published in the series 'Enquêtes et recherches statistiques: travaux en cours').

| 30–39%<br>(13 countries) | 40–49%<br>(13 countries) | 50–59%<br>(15 countries) |
|---|---|---|
| Botswana | Bahrain | Argentina |
| Brazil | Cyprus | Burma |
| Colombia | Ecuador | Chile |
| Congo | Gabon | Costa Rica |
| Dominican Republic | Jordan | Cuba |
| El Salvador | Kuwait | Jamaica |
| Ghana | Lebanon | Lesotho |
| Honduras | Malaysia | Mongolia |
| Nicaragua | Mauritius | Panama |
| Swaziland | Mexico | Philippines |
| Thailand | Paraguay | Republic of Korea |
| Tunisia | Peru | Singapore |
| Turkey | Venezuela | Sri Lanka |
| | | Trinidad and Tobago |
| | | Uruguay |

## DISTRIBUTION OF DEVELOPING COUNTRIES BY ENROLMENT RATIO OF BOYS AGED BETWEEN 6 AND 23 YEARS, 1965

| Under 10% (8 countries) | 10–19% (12 countries) | 20–29% (14 countries) | 30–39% (20 countries) |
|---|---|---|---|
| Bhutan | Afghanistan | Bangladesh | Algeria |
| Ethiopia | Angola | Benin | Brazil |
| Mauritania | Burundi | Botswana | Central African |
| Niger | Gambia | Burma | Empire |
| Oman | Guinea | Chad | Colombia |
| Somalia | Guinea-Bissau | Guatemala | Dominican |
| Upper Volta | Mali | Haiti | Republic |
| Yemen | Mozambique | Liberia | El Salvador |
| | Nepal | Malawi | Equatorial |
| | Nigeria | Pakistan | Guinea |
| | Saudi Arabia | Senegal | Honduras |
| | Sudan | Sierra Leone | Indonesia |
| | | United Republic | Ivory Coast |
| | | of Tanzania | Kenya |
| | | Democratic | Lesotho |
| | | Yemen | Madagascar |
| | | | Morocco |
| | | | Nicaragua |
| | | | Rwanda |
| | | | Swaziland |
| | | | Togo |
| | | | Uganda |
| | | | Zambia |

*Source:* As Appendix III.

| 40–49%<br>(14 countries) | 50–59%<br>(19 countries) | 60–69%<br>(8 countries) |
|---|---|---|
| Bolivia | Argentina | Bahrain |
| Cyprus | Chile | Guyana |
| Ecuador | Congo | Lebanon |
| Egypt | Costa Rica | Singapore |
| India | Cuba | Republic of Korea |
| Iran | Gabon | Syrian Arab Republic |
| Mexico | Ghana | Trinidad and Tobago |
| Mongolia | Iraq | Tunisia |
| Paraguay | Jamaica | |
| Thailand | Jordan | |
| Turkey | Kuwait | |
| United Republic | Libyan Arab | |
| of Cameroon | Jamahiriya | |
| Venezuela | Malaysia | |
| Zaire | Mauritius | |
| | Panama | |
| | Peru | |
| | Philippines | |
| | Sri Lanka | |
| | Uruguay | |

# DISTRIBUTION OF DEVELOPING COUNTRIES BY ENROLMENT RATIO OF GIRLS AGED BETWEEN 6 AND 23 YEARS, 1975

| Under 10% (11 countries) | 10–19% (16 countries) | 20–29% (11 countries) | 30–39% (13 countries) |
|---|---|---|---|
| Afghanistan | Bangladesh | Angola | Algeria |
| Bhutan | Benin | Central African | Burma |
| Burundi | Gambia | Empire | Egypt |
| Chad | Guinea | Democratic | Equatorial |
| Ethiopia | Guinea-Bissau | Yemen | Guinea |
| Mali | Haiti | Guatemala | Ghana |
| Mauritania | Morocco | India | Indonesia |
| Nepal | Mozambique | Ivory Coast | Iran |
| Niger | Nigeria | Liberia | Iraq |
| Upper Volta | Oman | Malawi | Madagascar |
| Yemen | Pakistan | Rwanda | Togo |
| | Saudi Arabia | Uganda | Tunisia |
| | Senegal | United Republic | Turkey |
| | Sierra Leone | of Tanzania | Zaire |
| | Somalia | | |
| | Sudan | | |

*Source:* As Appendix III.

| 40–49%<br>(14 countries) | 50–59%<br>(19 countries) | 60–69%<br>(8 countries) | 70% and over<br>(3 countries) |
|---|---|---|---|
| Bolivia | Bahrain | Argentina | Chile |
| Botswana | Brazil | Congo | Gabon |
| Colombia | Costa Rica | Cuba | Panama |
| Cyprus | Dominican | Jamaica | |
| El Salvador | Republic | Lesotho | |
| Honduras | Ecuador | Libyan Arab | |
| Jordan | Guyana | Jamahiriya | |
| Nicaragua | Kenya | Peru | |
| Paraguay | Kuwait | Trinidad | |
| Sri Lanka | Lebanon | and Tobago | |
| Syrian Arab | Malaysia | | |
| Republic | Mauritius | | |
| Thailand | Mexico | | |
| United Republic | Philippines | | |
| of Cameroon | Republic of | | |
| Zambia | Korea | | |
| | Singapore | | |
| | Swaziland | | |
| | Uruguay | | |
| | Venezuela | | |

## DISTRIBUTION OF DEVELOPING COUNTRIES BY ENROLMENT RATIO OF BOYS AGED BETWEEN 6 AND 23 YEARS, 1975

| Under 10% (3 countries) | 10–19% (6 countries) | 20–29% (13 countries) | 30–39% (11 countries) |
|---|---|---|---|
| Bhutan | Afghanistan | Chad | Angola |
| Niger | Burundi | Gambia | Benin |
| Upper Volta | Ethiopia | Guinea | Botswana |
| | Mali | Haiti | Burma |
| | Mauritania | Mozambique | Guatemala |
| | Yemen | Nepal | Liberia |
| | | Nigeria | Morocco |
| | | Oman | Pakistan |
| | | Rwanda | Saudi Arabia |
| | | Senegal | Uganda |
| | | Sierra Leone | United Republic |
| | | Somalia | of Tanzania |
| | | Sudan | |

*Source:* As Appendix III.

| 40–49%<br>(17 countries) | 50–59%<br>(26 countries) | 60–69%<br>(13 countries) | 70% and over<br>(7 countries) |
|---|---|---|---|
| Bangladesh | Algeria | Argentina | Chile |
| Central African | Bolivia | Bahrain | Congo |
| Empire | Brazil | Cuba | Gabon |
| Colombia | Costa Rica | Ecuador | Lebanon |
| Cyprus | Democratic | Iraq | Libyan Arab |
| El Salvador | Yemen | Jamaica | Jamahiriya |
| Equatorial | Dominican | Kenya | Panama |
| Guinea | Republic | Martinique | Syrian Arab |
| Ghana | Egypt | Mexico | Republic |
| Guinea-Bissau | Guyana | Peru | |
| Honduras | Iran | Republic | |
| India | Ivory Coast | of Korea | |
| Indonesia | Jordan | Togo | |
| Lesotho | Kuwait | Trinidad and | |
| Madagascar | Malaysia | Tobago | |
| Malawi | Mauritius | | |
| Nicaragua | Mongolia | | |
| Sri Lanka | Paraguay | | |
| Thailand | Philippines | | |
| | Singapore | | |
| | Swaziland | | |
| | Tunisia | | |
| | Turkey | | |
| | United Republic | | |
| | of Cameroon | | |
| | Uruguay | | |
| | Venezuela | | |
| | Zaire | | |
| | Zambia | | |

161

COMPARISON BY YEAR OF STUDY OF
AND DROP-OUT RATES
AND GIRLS (F)

| State and year | 1 | | 2 | | 3 | |
|---|---|---|---|---|---|---|
| | M | F | M | F | M | F |
| **Argentina (1970)** | | | | | | |
| Repetition | 23.6 | 20.0 | 13.5 | 10.7 | 11.2 | 9.0 |
| Promotion | 67.8 | 72.2 | 82.1 | 86.0 | 83.5 | 86.1 |
| Drop-out | 8.6 | 7.9 | 4.4 | 3.4 | 5.3 | 5.0 |
| **Austria (1971)** | | | | | | |
| Repetition | 6.1 | 4.6 | 6.4 | 4.6 | 6.0 | 3.4 |
| Promotion | 89.0 | 92.1 | 92.1 | 94.7 | 93.6 | 96.5 |
| Drop-out | 5.0 | 3.3 | 1.4 | 0.8 | 0.4 | 0.1 |
| **Belgium (1974)** | | | | | | |
| Repetition | 13.4 | 14.1 | 20.5 | 19.1 | 24.7 | 23.5 |
| Promotion | 74.4 | 76.1 | 73.0 | 73.9 | 73.0 | 74.3 |
| Drop-out | 12.2 | 9.9 | 6.5 | 7.1 | 2.3 | 2.2 |
| **Benin (1974)** | | | | | | |
| Repetition | 17.5 | 18.2 | 16.2 | 18.4 | 21.6 | 23.5 |
| Promotion | 61.8 | 59.3 | 71.1 | 69.3 | 69.5 | 64.4 |
| Drop-out | 20.7 | 22.6 | 12.7 | 12.3 | 8.9 | 12.1 |
| **Brazil (1973)** | | | | | | |
| Repetition | 24.6 | 22.0 | 17.7 | 15.2 | 11.4 | 10.0 |
| Promotion | 39.7 | 43.8 | 69.2 | 73.1 | 74.8 | 77.5 |
| Drop-out | 35.7 | 34.2 | 13.1 | 11.8 | 13.8 | 12.6 |
| **Burma (1972)** | | | | | | |
| Repetition | 30.4 | 30.7 | 17.4 | 18.5 | 17.2 | 16.9 |
| Promotion | 60.9 | 59.3 | 61.2 | 60.3 | 62.5 | 56.9 |
| Drop-out | 8.7 | 10.0 | 21.4 | 21.2 | 20.3 | 26.1 |
| **Central African Empire (1974)** | | | | | | |
| Repetition | 40.3 | 40.9 | 31.8 | 35.6 | 32.9 | 34.2 |
| Promotion | 50.7 | 56.7 | 56.3 | 59.3 | 55.6 | 54.7 |
| Drop-out | 9.0 | 2.4 | 11.9 | 5.1 | 11.5 | 11.0 |

# REPETITION, PROMOTION (PERCENTAGES) AMONG BOYS(M) IN FORTY-THREE COUNTRIES

| Year of study and sex of pupil | | | | | | | | | | | |
|---|---|---|---|---|---|---|---|---|---|---|---|
| 4 | | 5 | | 6 | | 7 | | 8 | | 9 | |
| M | F | M | F | M | F | M | F | M | F | M | F |
| 8.7 | 6.4 | 6.3 | 4.5 | 4.1 | 3.0 | 1.5 | 1.2 | | | | |
| 84.6 | 88.0 | 85.2 | 88.7 | 87.0 | 90.5 | | | | | | |
| 6.7 | 5.6 | 8.5 | 6.8 | 8.9 | 6.6 | | | | | | |
| 4.8 | 3.3 | | | | | | | | | | |
| 95.2 | 96.7 | | | | | | | | | | |
| 25.9 | 24.1 | 33.7 | 27.2 | 29.5 | 27.4 | | | | | | |
| 66.5 | 70.6 | 68.1 | 69.0 | | | | | | | | |
| 7.6 | 5.3 | —1.8 | 3.8 | | | | | | | | |
| 20.0 | 24.1 | 27.8 | 31.7 | 43.2 | 46.8 | | | | | | |
| 76.6 | 68.5 | 70.1 | 60.0 | | | | | | | | |
| 3.4 | 7.4 | 2.1 | 8.3 | | | | | | | | |
| 10.9 | 9.8 | 14.8 | 11.0 | 13.9 | 10.9 | 11.4 | 9.3 | 8.2 | 6.3 | | |
| 80.9 | 78.2 | 72.5 | 79.1 | 80.6 | 86.6 | 83.4 | 88.7 | | | | |
| 8.2 | 12.5 | 12.7 | 9.9 | 5.4 | 2.5 | 5.3 | 2.0 | | | | |
| 15.3 | 17.7 | 14.3 | 14.0 | | | | | | | | |
| 60.6 | 55.8 | | | | | | | | | | |
| 24.1 | 26.5 | | | | | | | | | | |
| | 32.4 | 27.7 | 30.3 | 48.4 | 47.7 | | | | | | |
| | 61.0 | 63.3 | 60.1 | | | | | | | | |
| | 6.6 | 8.5 | 9.6 | | | | | | | | |

| State and year | 1 | | 2 | | 3 | |
|---|---|---|---|---|---|---|
| | M | F | M | F | M | F |
| **Chad (1974)** | | | | | | |
| Repetition | 46.4 | 44.7 | 36.5 | 37.2 | 34.2 | 40.8 |
| Promotion | 40.3 | 36.9 | 60.3 | 51.6 | 53.3 | 46.7 |
| Drop-out | 13.3 | 18.4 | 3.1 | 11.2 | 12.5 | 12.5 |
| **Chile (1973)** | | | | | | |
| Repetition | 20.2 | 17.2 | 16.6 | 13.3 | 14.0 | 10.8 |
| Promotion | 71.4 | 74.1 | 79.1 | 82.6 | 81.7 | 85.3 |
| Drop-out | 8.4 | 8.7 | 4.2 | 4.1 | 4.3 | 4.0 |
| **Colombia (1973)** | | | | | | |
| Repetition | 21.6 | 18.6 | 16.4 | 15.1 | 14.4 | 12.7 |
| Promotion | 51.3 | 58.0 | 68.8 | 69.3 | 61.1 | 65.1 |
| Drop-out | 27.2 | 23.4 | 14.8 | 15.6 | 24.5 | 22.2 |
| **Costa Rica (1971)** | | | | | | |
| Repetition | 11.9 | 9.4 | 8.1 | 6.3 | 6.8 | 5.4 |
| Promotion | 81.1 | 84.9 | 85.9 | 89.9 | 86.9 | 89.5 |
| Drop-out | 7.1 | 5.7 | 6.0 | 3.8 | 6.3 | 5.2 |
| **Cyprus (1974)** | | | | | | |
| Repetition | 5.4 | 3.5 | 1.2 | 1.2 | 0.1 | 0.0 |
| Promotion | 92.1 | 94.5 | 97.6 | 98.5 | 99.2 | 98.2 |
| Drop-out | 2.6 | 2.0 | 1.1 | 0.3 | 0.7 | 1.6 |
| **Czechoslovakia (1974)** | | | | | | |
| Repetition | 0.5 | 0.4 | 2.0 | 1.7 | 1.2 | 0.8 |
| Promotion | 98.5 | 98.2 | 96.4 | 97.2 | 98.2 | 98.6 |
| Drop-out | 1.0 | 1.4 | 1.6 | 1.0 | 0.7 | 0.6 |
| **Dominican Republic(1969)** | | | | | | |
| Repetition | 37.4 | 33.1 | 21.4 | 19.1 | 18.3 | 17.2 |
| Promotion | 39.6 | 43.6 | 64.0 | 69.9 | 62.9 | 64.2 |
| Drop-out | 23.0 | 23.2 | 14.6 | 11.1 | 18.8 | 18.6 |
| **Ecuador (1972)** | | | | | | |
| Repetition | 18.3 | 17.7 | 15.1 | 14.9 | 12.0 | 1 |
| Promotion | 64.6 | 64.7 | 78.3 | 78.9 | 81.8 | |
| Drop-out | 17.1 | 17.6 | 6.5 | 6.1 | 6.3 | |

| Year of study and sex of pupil | | | | | | | | | | | |
|---|---|---|---|---|---|---|---|---|---|---|---|
| 4 | | 5 | | 6 | | 7 | | 8 | | 9 | |
| M | F | M | F | M | F | M | F | M | F | M | F |
| 30.2 | 32.7 | 35.0 | 35.0 | 66.4 | 60.8 | | | | | | |
| 66.8 | 62.4 | 69.4 | 56.7 | | | | | | | | |
| 3.0 | 4.9 | —4.4 | 8.3 | | | | | | | | |
| 11.7 | 9.3 | 11.0 | 8.4 | 9.4 | 6.9 | 10.8 | 7.1 | 6.5 | 4.6 | | |
| 82.5 | 85.3 | 82.9 | 85.3 | 80.7 | 82.7 | 76.5 | 83.6 | | | | |
| 5.8 | 5.4 | 6.1 | 6.3 | 9.9 | 10.5 | 12.7 | 9.3 | | | | |
| 12.4 | 10.6 | 9.1 | 7.1 | | | | | | | | |
| 78.5 | 82.3 | | | | | | | | | | |
| 9.1 | 7.1 | | | | | | | | | | |
| 4.6 | 3.8 | 3.0 | 2.4 | 1.6 | 1.3 | | | | | | |
| 88.3 | 89.3 | 90.8 | 92.6 | | | | | | | | |
| 7.1 | 6.9 | 6.2 | 5.0 | | | | | | | | |
| 0.1 | 0.1 | 0.1 | 0.1 | 0.1 | 0.1 | | | | | | |
| 99.2 | 99.0 | 100.5 | 99.5 | 0.6 | 0.7 | | | | | | |
| 0.8 | 0.9 | —0.6 | 0.4 | 99.3 | 99.2 | | | | | | |
| 1.2 | 0.7 | 0.9 | 0.5 | 1.3 | 0.6 | 1.2 | 0.5 | 0.6 | 0.3 | 0.0 | 0.1 |
| 97.7 | 98.9 | 97.9 | 99.0 | 97.0 | 98.4 | 95.0 | 97.2 | 88.6 | 90.7 | | |
| 1.1 | 0.4 | 1.1 | 0.5 | 1.7 | 1.0 | 3.8 | 2.4 | 10.8 | 9.0 | | |
| 14.6 | 13.8 | 11.3 | 10.9 | 7.0 | 6.8 | | | | | | |
| 69.1 | 70.7 | 72.9 | 77.9 | | | | | | | | |
| 16.3 | 15.5 | 15.8 | 11.2 | | | | | | | | |
| 11.7 | 12.5 | 10.5 | 10.1 | 10.0 | 9.9 | | | | | | |
| 78.8 | 78.8 | 86.9 | 85.8 | | | | | | | | |
| 9.5 | 8.7 | 2.6 | 4.1 | | | | | | | | |

| State and year | 1 | | 2 | | 3 | |
|---|---|---|---|---|---|---|
| | M | F | M | F | M | F |
| **France (1970)** | | | | | | |
| Repetition | 18.1 | 14.5 | 11.2 | 9.1 | 10.4 | 8.6 |
| Promotion | 77.5 | 82.1 | 86.2 | 88.8 | 89.6 | 91.9 |
| Drop-out | 4.4 | 3.4 | 2.6 | 2.0 | 0.0 | 0.0 |
| **Ghana (1974)** | | | | | | |
| Repetition | 5.4 | 5.5 | 2.2 | 2.5 | 1.7 | 1.9 |
| Promotion | 94.0 | 88.5 | 99.6 | 98.2 | 99.0 | 95.6 |
| Drop-out | 0.5 | 6.0 | —1.8 | —0.7 | —0.8 | 2.4 |
| **Greece (1972)** | | | | | | |
| Repetition | 9.2 | 7.2 | 5.4 | 4.1 | 4.9 | 3.3 |
| Promotion | 88.9 | 90.6 | 93.8 | 95.3 | 94.1 | 95.6 |
| Drop-out | 1.9 | 2.2 | 0.9 | 0.6 | 1.0 | 1.0 |
| **Guatemala (1968)** | | | | | | |
| Repetition | 26.7 | 26.1 | 13.9 | 13.2 | 12.6 | 12.4 |
| Promotion | 49.7 | 48.9 | 66.7 | 67.6 | 63.0 | 65.8 |
| Drop-out | 23.6 | 25.1 | 19.5 | 19.2 | 24.4 | 21.8 |
| **Hungary (1974)** | | | | | | |
| Repetition | 6.1 | 4.5 | 3.4 | 2.4 | 3.0 | 1.8 |
| Promotion | 91.3 | 92.5 | 96.0 | 97.1 | 96.2 | 97.8 |
| Drop-out | 2.6 | 3.0 | 0.6 | 0.5 | 0.8 | 0.4 |
| **India (1969)** | | | | | | |
| Repetition | 26.4 | 26.4 | 20.2 | 20.6 | 18.5 | 19.5 |
| Promotion | 50.7 | 48.7 | 68.1 | 64.7 | 70.6 | 66.1 |
| Drop-out | 22.9 | 24.9 | 11.7 | 14.7 | 10.9 | 14.5 |
| **Iran (1969)** | | | | | | |
| Repetition | 12.8 | 7.6 | 13.9 | 8.4 | 10.0 | 6.5 |
| Promotion | 77.4 | 78.7 | 81.4 | 86.0 | 86.1 | 89.4 |
| Drop-out | 9.8 | 13.8 | 4.7 | 5.7 | 3.9 | 4.1 |
| **Iraq (1972)** | | | | | | |
| Repetition | 22.3 | 20.9 | 16.6 | 17.5 | 13.6 | 14.5 |
| Promotion | 72.0 | 71.1 | 81.2 | 78.3 | 85.6 | 82.7 |
| Drop-out | 5.7 | 6.4 | 2.2 | 2.8 | 0.8 | 1.3 |

| Year of study and sex of pupil | | | | | | | | | | | |
|---|---|---|---|---|---|---|---|---|---|---|---|
| 4 | | 5 | | 6 | | 7 | | 8 | | 9 | |
| M | F | M | F | M | F | M | F | M | F | M | F |
| 11.0 | 9.5 | 14.7 | 13.0 | 7.2 | 6.2 | | | | | | |
| 82.6 | 85.9 | | | | | | | | | | |
| 6.4 | 4.6 | | | | | | | | | | |
| 1.6 | 1.7 | 1.2 | 1.5 | | 1.2 | | | | | | |
| 97.4 | 95.6 | 99.5 | 96.0 | | | | | | | | |
| 1.0 | 0.3 | —0.8 | 0.2 | | | | | | | | |
| 3.1 | 1.9 | 3.0 | 1.8 | 1.3 | 0.9 | | | | | | |
| 96.5 | 97.2 | 96.3 | 96.6 | | | | | | | | |
| 0.5 | 0.9 | 0.7 | 1.7 | | | | | | | | |
| 8.6 | 8.4 | 5.9 | 5.5 | 2.1 | 2.1 | | | | | | |
| 76.5 | 76.4 | 83.0 | 86.0 | | | | | | | | |
| 14.9 | 15.2 | 11.0 | 8.5 | | | | | | | | |
| 2.2 | 1.3 | 4.7 | 2.8 | 3.3 | 2.0 | 2.5 | 1.3 | 0.4 | 0.2 | | |
| 97.5 | 97.9 | 93.9 | 96.0 | 95.0 | 96.5 | 94.5 | 97.2 | | | | |
| 0.3 | 0.8 | 1.4 | 1.2 | 1.7 | 1.5 | 3.0 | 1.5 | | | | |
| 17.1 | 18.5 | 15.5 | 17.3 | | | | | | | | |
| 72.7 | 66.2 | | | | | | | | | | |
| 10.2 | 15.3 | 84.5 | 82.7 | | | | | | | | |
| 8.3 | 6.7 | 8.0 | 5.9 | 11.1 | 5.2 | | | | | | |
| 87.0 | 89.3 | 86.1 | 87.5 | | | | | | | | |
| 4.7 | 4.0 | 6.0 | 6.6 | | | | | | | | |
| 19.1 | 21.2 | 34.5 | 33.6 | 20.5 | 12.4 | | | | | | |
| 76.7 | 71.7 | 58.9 | 57.9 | | | | | | | | |
| 4.3 | 5.1 | 6.7 | 7.2 | | | | | | | | |

| State and year | 1 | | 2 | | 3 | |
|---|---|---|---|---|---|---|
| | M | F | M | F | M | F |
| **Italy (1972)** | | | | | | |
| Repetition | 7.5 | 5.6 | 6.1 | 4.3 | 4.7 | 3.4 |
| Promotion | 96.6 | 98.7 | 93.4 | 95.5 | 94.4 | 95.4 |
| Drop-out | —4.2 | —4.3 | 0.5 | 0.3 | 1.0 | 1.2 |
| **Ivory Coast (1972)** | | | | | | |
| Repetition | 22.9 | 22.5 | 21.1 | 21.2 | 22.9 | 23.1 |
| Promotion | 72.8 | 69.5 | 77.9 | 75.6 | 73.8 | 70.5 |
| Drop-out | 4.3 | 7.9 | 1.0 | 3.2 | 3.3 | 6.4 |
| **Jordan (1974)** | | | | | | |
| Repetition | 0.1 | 0.1 | 0.2 | 0.3 | 5.8 | 6.4 |
| Promotion | 93.3 | 94.6 | 99.5 | 99.1 | 93.2 | 91.8 |
| Drop-out | 6.7 | 5.3 | 0.3 | 0.6 | 1.0 | 1.8 |
| **Malta (1970)** | | | | | | |
| Repetition | 1.0 | 1.2 | 1.2 | 1.1 | 0.8 | 0.4 |
| Promotion | 75.3 | 77.7 | 104.5 | 105.2 | 101.2 | 99.8 |
| Drop-out | 23.7 | 21.2 | —5.8 | —6.3 | —2.0 | —0.1 |
| **Mexico (1974)** | | | | | | |
| Repetition | 18.8 | 16.4 | 13.0 | 11.1 | 11.5 | 10.1 |
| Promotion | 68.0 | 66.6 | 78.4 | 75.1 | 79.9 | 79.0 |
| Drop-out | 13.2 | 17.0 | 8.6 | 13.8 | 8.6 | 13.8 |
| **Morocco (1973)** | | | | | | |
| Repetition | 24.7 | 25.2 | 22.2 | 21.6 | 28.6 | 28.6 |
| Promotion | 66.9 | 66.9 | 74.4 | 75.5 | 67.2 | 66.9 |
| Drop-out | 8.3 | 7.9 | —3.4 | 2.9 | 4.2 | 4.5 |
| **Netherlands (1974)** | | | | | | |
| Repetition | 7.1 | 4.3 | 3.7 | 2.8 | 2.2 | 2.0 |
| Promotion | 91.7 | 95.1 | 95.2 | 96.8 | 97.3 | 97.9 |
| Drop-out | 1.3 | 0.5 | 1.1 | 0.3 | 0.5 | 0.1 |
| **Nicaragua (1972)** | | | | | | |
| Repetition | 17.0 | 16.1 | 11.9 | 11.0 | 10.1 | 9.1 |
| Promotion | 46.7 | 50.1 | 72.0 | 74.6 | 73.1 | 75.1 |
| Drop-out | 36.3 | 33.8 | 16.1 | 14.5 | 16.8 | 15.8 |

| Year of study and sex of pupil | | | | | | | | | | | |
|---|---|---|---|---|---|---|---|---|---|---|---|
| 4 | | 5 | | 6 | | 7 | | 8 | | 9 | |
| M | F | M | F | M | F | M | F | M | F | M | F |
| 4.3 | 3.1 | 2.9 | 2.2 | | | | | | | | |
| 94.4 | 95.5 | | | | | | | | | | |
| 1.3 | 1.4 | | | | | | | | | | |
| 22.7 | 22.7 | 29.9 | 30.4 | 50.1 | 50.9 | | | | | | |
| 79.0 | 71.9 | 75.0 | 60.0 | | | | | | | | |
| —1.7 | 5.4 | —4.9 | 9.6 | | | | | | | | |
| 7.9 | 8.8 | 6.3 | 6.9 | 4.8 | 5.3 | | | | | | |
| 90.3 | 87.9 | 90.0 | 88.2 | | | | | | | | |
| 1.8 | 3.2 | 3.7 | 4.9 | | | | | | | | |
| 0.6 | 0.3 | 1.4 | 0.4 | 0.9 | 1.2 | 0.4 | 0.4 | 3.0 | 2.5 | | |
| 96.2 | 99.2 | 101.1 | 102.2 | | | | | | | | |
| 3.2 | 0.5 | —2.5 | —2.6 | | | | | | | | |
| 9.5 | 8.8 | 7.8 | 7.5 | | 2.4 | | | | | | |
| 79.2 | 82.3 | 85.5 | 92.5 | | | | | | | | |
| 8.6 | 10.9 | 11.3 | 8.9 | 6.7 | | | | | | | |
| 32.8 | 32.5 | 49.3 | 49.3 | | | | | | | | |
| 63.1 | 62.4 | | | | | | | | | | |
| 4.1 | 5.1 | | | | | | | | | | |
| 1.8 | 1.8 | 1.3 | 1.3 | 0.8 | 0.8 | | | | | | |
| 98.2 | 98.3 | 97.5 | 97.6 | | | | | | | | |
| 0.0 | 0.0 | 1.2 | 1.0 | | | | | | | | |
| 8.4 | 7.4 | 6.1 | 5.5 | 3.4 | 2.7 | | | | | | |
| .1 | 77.7 | 80.7 | 82.3 | | | | | | | | |
| 6 | 14.9 | 13.2 | 12.2 | | | | | | | | |

| State and year | 1 | | 2 | | 3 | |
|---|---|---|---|---|---|---|
| | M | F | M | F | M | F |
| **Oman (1973)** | | | | | | |
| Repetition | 8.6 | 7.5 | 9.2 | 17.1 | 14.4 | 16.4 |
| Promotion | 79.1 | 83.3 | 85.6 | 81.9 | 78.2 | 68.3 |
| Drop-out | 12.3 | 9.2 | 5.2 | 1.5 | 7.5 | 15.3 |
| **Panama (1974)** | | | | | | |
| Repetition | 22.5 | 18.4 | 19.3 | 13.8 | 15.5 | 11.9 |
| Promotion | 70.3 | 74.7 | 78.2 | 82.2 | 80.0 | 84.8 |
| Drop-out | 7.2 | 6.9 | 2.5 | 4.0 | 4.5 | 3.3 |
| **Paraguay (1973)** | | | | | | |
| Repetition | 26.8 | 23.4 | 22.1 | 18.0 | 17.2 | 14.6 |
| Promotion | 62.1 | 64.9 | 56.6 | 71.2 | 68.6 | 71.3 |
| Drop-out | 11.1 | 11.8 | 11.3 | 10.8 | 14.3 | 14.1 |
| **Portugal (1973)** | | | | | | |
| Repetition | 36.5 | 31.6 | 26.0 | 21.3 | 20.4 | 16.0 |
| Promotion | 63.3 | 69.0 | 72.0 | 78.1 | 75.7 | 80.9 |
| Drop-out | 0.3 | —0.6 | 2.0 | 0.7 | 4.0 | 3.1 |
| **Saudi Arabia (1973)** | | | | | | |
| Repetition | 21.1 | 14.5 | 15.9 | 12.0 | 17.0 | 11.9 |
| Promotion | 73.1 | 81.5 | 82.9 | 87.1 | 82.4 | 86.9 |
| Drop-out | 5.8 | 4.0 | 1.2 | 0.9 | 0.6 | 1.1 |
| **Singapore (1974)** | | | | | | |
| Repetition | 0.0 | 0.0 | 0.1 | 0.1 | 3.0 | 1.8 |
| Promotion | 100.0 | 99.8 | 100.0 | 100.1 | 96.3 | 97.2 |
| Drop-out | 0.0 | 0.2 | —0.4 | 0.2 | 0.7 | 1.0 |
| **Sri Lanka (1975)** | | | | | | |
| Repetition | | 14.8 | | 12.3 | | 13.7 |
| Promotion | | 84.2 | | 84.5 | | 79.9 |
| Drop-out | | 1.1 | | 3.2 | | 6.5 |
| **Syrian Arab Republic (1973)** | | | | | | |
| Repetition | 12.2 | 12.8 | 11.1 | 11.2 | 10.5 | 10 |
| Promotion | 85.4 | 82.9 | 87.6 | 84.9 | 87.1 | 8 |
| Drop-out | 2.5 | 4.3 | 1.3 | 4.0 | 2.3 | |

Year of study and sez of pnpil

| 4 | | 5 | | 6 | | 7 | | 8 | | 9 | |
|---|---|---|---|---|---|---|---|---|---|---|---|
| M | F | M | F | M | F | M | F | M | F | M | F |
| 14.8 | 30.7 | 12.8 | 13.9 | 10.0 | 12.4 | | | | | | |
| 68.6 | 49.7 | 89.5 | 42.3 | | | | | | | | |
| 16.6 | 19.7 | —2.3 | 43.8 | | | | | | | | |
| 11.0 | 7.8 | 7.8 | 5.5 | 2.7 | 1.9 | | | | | | |
| 85.2 | 87.7 | 88.7 | 90.4 | 12.5 | 9.3 | | | | | | |
| 3.8 | 4.6 | 3.6 | 4.0 | 84.8 | 88.8 | | | | | | |
| 12.8 | 9.4 | 7.9 | 5.6 | 4.5 | 2.7 | | | | | | |
| 70.5 | 73.6 | 73.9 | 76.8 | | | | | | | | |
| 16.7 | 17.0 | 18.3 | 17.5 | | | | | | | | |
| 21.3 | 19.3 | 5.5 | 4.6 | 1.9 | 1.0 | | | | | | |
| } 75.5 | } 76.9 | 51.3 | 55.1 | | | | | | | | |
| | | 43.2 | 40.4 | | | | | | | | |
| 27.4 | 19.5 | 18.0 | 13.4 | 11.6 | 4.8 | | | | | | |
| 68.6 | 77.3 | 76.7 | 83.0 | | | | | | | | |
| 4.0 | 3.2 | 5.3 | 3.6 | | | | | | | | |
| 4.1 | 2.3 | 5.1 | 2.9 | 33.5 | 21.4 | | | | | | |
| 94.8 | 96.6 | 92.7 | 94.4 | | | | | | | | |
| 1.1 | 1.1 | 2.2 | 2.7 | | | | | | | | |
| | 15.1 | | 11.5 | | | | | | | | |
| | 75.4 | | | | | | | | | | |
| | 9.5 | | | | | | | | | | |
| 9.6 | 9.4 | 7.7 | 7.4 | 10.3 | 5.1 | | | | | | |
| .3 | 82.5 | 87.5 | 82.4 | | | | | | | | |
| 1 | 8.1 | 4.8 | 10.1 | | | | | | | | |

| State and year | 1 | | 2 | | 3 | |
|---|---|---|---|---|---|---|
| | M | F | M | F | M | F |
| **Thailand (1974)** | | | | | | |
| Repetition | 20.4 | 17.9 | 12.9 | 10.2 | 12.3 | 9.5 |
| Promotion | 72.3 | 75.0 | 85.2 | 87.8 | 84.2 | 87.1 |
| Drop-out | 7.3 | 7.0 | 1.9 | 2.1 | 3.5 | 3.4 |
| **United Arab Emirates (1975)** | | | | | | |
| Repetition | 12.1 | 15.0 | 14.8 | 16.1 | 15.6 | 14.6 |
| Promotion | 90.3 | 91.2 | 87.4 | 86.6 | 85.7 | 88.1 |
| Drop-out | —2.4 | —6.2 | —2.3 | —2.7 | —1.3 | —2.7 |
| **United Republic of Cameroon (1972)** | | | | | | |
| Repetition | 33.9 | 32.9 | 25.8 | 24.8 | 26.0 | 25.4 |
| Promotion | 51.4 | 52.7 | 70.0 | 71.3 | 68.0 | 67.4 |
| Drop-out | 14.7 | 14.4 | 4.2 | 3.9 | 6.0 | 7.2 |
| **Zambia (1973)** | | | | | | |
| Repetition | 0.5 | 0.4 | 0.6 | 0.6 | 0.9 | 0.9 |
| Promotion | 102.3 | 100.8 | 102.1 | 98.8 | 101.5 | 97.3 |
| Drop-out | —2.9 | —1.3 | —2.7 | 0.6 | —2.5 | 1.7 |

*Source:* Unesco Office of Statistics.

| Year of study and sex of pupil | | | | | | | | | | | |
|---|---|---|---|---|---|---|---|---|---|---|---|
| 4 | | 5 | | 6 | | 7 | | 8 | | 9 | |
| M | F | M | F | M | F | M | F | M | F | M | F |
| 4.1 | 3.3 | 8.1 | 7.4 | 4.1 | 3.5 | 1.9 | 1.5 | | | | |
| 54.5 | 48.3 | 83.3 | 83.3 | 89.5 | 90.7 | | | | | | |
| 41.4 | 48.3 | 8.5 | 9.4 | 6.3 | 5.8 | | | | | | |
| 20.3 | 19.7 | 18.9 | 15.7 | 9.2 | 7.1 | | | | | | |
| 78.0 | 82.0 | 75.9 | 81.8 | | | | | | | | |
| 1.7 | —1.7 | 5.2 | 2.5 | | | | | | | | |
| 20.5 | 20.2 | 24.8 | 25.0 | 38.5 | 35.8 | 13.9 | 14.1 | | | | |
| 73.8 | 71.3 | 72.2 | 66.7 | 10.9 | 10.0 | | | | | | |
| 5.7 | 8.5 | 3.0 | 8.3 | 50.7 | 54.2 | | | | | | |
| 4.2 | 3.4 | 0.5 | 0.5 | 1.2 | 1.2 | 10.1 | 8.8 | | | | |
| 81.3 | 74.4 | 102.3 | 95.7 | 100.3 | 87.7 | | | | | | |
| 14.5 | 22.2 | —2.8 | 3.8 | —1.6 | 11.1 | | | | | | |

RECOMMENDATION NO. 66
CONCERNING THE IMPROVED
EFFECTIVENESS OF EDUCATIONAL
SYSTEMS PARTICULARLY THROUGH
REDUCTION OF WASTAGE
AT ALL LEVELS OF INSTRUCTION

PREAMBLE

The International Conference on Education convened in Geneva by the United Nations Educational, Scientific and Cultural Organization, having assembled on the first of July nineteen hundred and seventy for its thirty-second session, adopts on the eighth of July nineteen hundred and seventy the following Recommendation

The Conference,
Considering Article 26 of the Universal Declaration of Human Rights (1948),
Considering the Declaration of the Rights of the Child (1959),
Considering the Convention and Recommendation against Discrimination in Education adopted by the General Conference of Unesco at its eleventh session (1960),
Considering the Recommendation concerning Technical and Vocational Education adopted by the General Conference of Unesco at its twelfth session (1962),
Considering the Recommendation concerning the Status of Teachers adopted by the Special Intergovernmental Conference on the Status of Teachers (1966),
Considering the Declaration of the Principles of International Cultural Co-operation adopted by the General Conference of Unesco at its fourteenth session (1966),
Considering the recommendations of the International Conference on Educational Planning (1968),
Considering that we are entering the Second Development Decade,
Considering that 1970 has been declared International Education Year,
Considering the relevant recommendations adopted by the International Conference on Public Education at its various sessions,
Considering that education has as its aim not only the inculcation of essential knowledge but also and principally the development of all aspects of the personality of the pupil and that teaching methods should be adapted to this end,
Considering that it is necessary that every pupil should be enabled to complete the cycle of education on which he embarks and, that within

the framework of life-long education, there should be adequate provision of continuing education for the early leaver,

Considering that most countries have been seriously concerned with some form of wastage, and that statistical analysis has shown clearly the extent and distribution of the phenomenon of wastage at various levels and points of the educational systems,

Considering that drop-outs often entail unproductive expenditure and that repetitions increase the cost of education thereby prejudicing both qualitative and quantitative improvement in education, to say nothing of the ill-effects that repetition may have upon pupils,

Considering that the improvement of the effectiveness of educational systems and particularly the reduction of wastage are essential both for ensuring for all the realization of the right to education and also in order to strengthen the contribution of education to social and economic development of the society,

Submits the following Recommendation to the Ministries of Education of the different countries:

BASIC PRINCIPLES

1. The measures to be taken to reduce educational wastage should be studied in the light of the following principles:
   (a) all aspects of the social and economic context and of the educational systems are relevant to wastage;
   (b) many factors contribute to wastage at the different levels of instruction. They vary widely from one country to another, particularly with the level of development. Broadly speaking, they fall into one of the following categories:
   the environment
      (i) home and community: geographical, social, economic or cultural constraints (distance from school, an unhelpful environment, linguistic differences, underdevelopment, public opinion, etc.),
      (ii) the school system (administration, organization, curricula, number and qualification of teachers, family-school relationship, buildings and equipment, etc.),
      the personality of the child (physical, mental, intellectual and moral factors, motivation, etc.)
   (c) factors associated with wastage usually occur in combination and require studies concerned with their interaction as well as with their independent effects. These studies should be based mainly on what has been learnt through experience in a particular context.
2. The reform of educational systems resulting from the evolution of civilization should encourage us to re-examine, in the light of the specific characteristics of each country, the question of curriculum reform (especially in the first years of the school course), the role of evaluation procedures and ways of organizing school and vocational

175

guidance with a view to reducing educational wastage and also failure to enter upon a working life successfully.

PRACTICAL MEASURES TO REDUCE SCHOOL WASTAGE

3. A number of measures should be taken, some of which should be of a general nature, aimed at improving the effectiveness of educational systems. These should effect a renewal of such systems by bringing them closer to life, to economic and social needs, and to individual aspirations. Other more specific steps should deal with the various factors influencing wastage.

4. The aims of education in a rapidly changing world should be redefined, taking into account the contribution which education must make to human, social and economic development and to the effective implementation of the right to education.

5. It seems desirable to keep the concept of the life-long education in mind, since this provides a link between education and life, and ensures that people's knowledge is constantly improved and that school and out-of-school education are properly co-ordinated. It seems desirable to overhaul educational structures in order to achieve greater flexibility and a better coherence between the various components of education, while ensuring maximum continuity within systems and facilitating transfer from one type or level to another.

6. Care should also be taken, when determining the content of education, to allow for the need not only to teach facts, but also to teach how to learn; basic instruction should have its proper place; new subjects should be included where necessary as knowledge progresses; an introduction to practical life and technology should be provided; and attention should be given to the inculcation of attitudes which will be beneficial in a working life.

7. It seems desirable that there should be continual improvement of the methods used in teaching and education in general, both by using modern information media and educational technology, and by applying the results of educational and psychological research so that the methods used are better suited to the child's needs.

8. It is essential to improve the pre-service and in-service training of teachers and their guidance, paying particular attention to their preparation for the new role they are to play, in view of the need for a new type of relationship between teachers and the taught and for a broad preparation for life.

9. It is important that selection procedures and methods used to test knowledge and assess school results should be reviewed, and that arbitrariness and subjectivity in these matters should be eliminated as far as possible; it seems desirable to adopt a positive attitude towards pupils and to take into account the affective and temperamental aspects of each pupil's personality. To this end it seems desirable to adopt measures to evaluate the efficiency of educational institutions as a whole.

10. It is essential to develop school counselling and vocational guidance services on a permanent basis, so as to supply the children, their families and the public with adequate information about the educational system and the opportunities it provides for achieving a better life in general and for employment.
11. There should be close co-operation between educational administrators, educators, school psychologists, careers advisers, doctors, social workers and parents.
12. There should be close co-operation between the school, the family and the community.
13. In order to offset certain social, economic and geographical handicaps, the following steps should be taken *inter alia*
    (a) the extension of free education at all levels and the extension and improvement of the school network and better distribution of schools, particular attention being paid to the needs of rural areas and minority groups;
    (b) the establishment of boarding schools, especially for children from sparsely populated areas;
    (c) the institution or expansion of social services or the application of a policy of assisting the family or child (canteens, free food or clothing, school transport allowances, nurseries open during parents' working hours, etc.);
    (d) the expansion of school health and medical services;
    (e) the expansion of pre-school education, especially in rural areas and the overcrowded areas in large towns;
    (f) the granting, on a more equitable basis, of more scholarships and educational allowances of various kinds as well as of grants for higher education which will free students from the need to take paid work that hinders their studies;
    (g) supervised study on a voluntary basis after school hours;
14. Systematic public information should be organized on a permanent basis to give parents an awareness of the importance of their children's attending schools.
15. Steps should be taken to make schooling compulsory; provide the facilities needed to cater for the enrolment of all children; and prevent foreseeable voluntary drop-out, particularly when this results from the working activities of minors.
16. Services should be set up or expanded to trace physically or mentally handicapped children and institutions should be founded for such children.
17. The teaching of the language of instruction should be improved, both as a subject and as a tool for the acquisition of knowledge.
18. Steps should be taken to eliminate those factors making for wastage which are connected with the use of a language other than the mother tongue as the vehicle of instruction.
19. Special attention should be given to the teaching of basic subjects in which wastage sometimes occurs—for instance, the mother tongue and mathematics.
20. Measures should be devised to reduce the rate of repetition in the

first years of the primary course, in which they appear to be particularly high.

21. In reviewing the content of education, provision should be made for new subjects closely related to life, the environment and work, in order to strengthen the pupils' motivation.

22. It is also desirable to deepen the child's interest in school through various extra-curricula and out-of-school activities.

23. School psychological services should be established or improved, and the role of the school psychologist should be redefined and expanded.

24. In the educational structure provision should be made for complementary forms of education which will enable children who have dropped out from school or who are seriously behind in their work to acquire more general knowledge and vocational or pre-vocational training, so that they may re-enter the educational system or enter the production sector.

25. A study should be made of the possibility and desirability of introducing, at the appropriate level, trade courses or preparatory courses for working life.

26. In reviewing the content and structures of education, a study should be made of the possibility of the school giving the pupil, at an appropriate age, practical experience of the world of work as part of his training for life.

27. The material conditions in which education is given—equipment, teaching materials, laboratories and libraries—should be improved.

28. The important factor of wastage resulting from excessively large classes should be eliminated by reducing the numbers in each class so that there is an appropriate pupil/teacher ratio in countries where circumstances allow of this, although this should not be done in those countries where it would make the school attendance situation worse. In such countries, educational authorities and research workers should devise ways of improving the efficiency of such classes, thus reducing wastage.

29. The results of experience gained by teachers and schools which have succeeded in reducing wastage considerably or even in eliminating it should be disseminated and widely applied.

30. In reforming educational systems and working out special measures to reduce wastage rates, account should be taken of the part that can be played by educational research and the science of education.

STUDIES TO BE CARRIED OUT

I. *Statistical studies*

31. The collection of data for national purposes should be standardized and organized systematically. To this end, reference should be made to the methods used in the Unesco survey on the statistical measurement of educational wastage (1969), in order to calculate drop-out and repetition rates and (or) to assess the effectiveness of educational

systems (although such methods might be improved) and use should if necessary be made of modern data-processing techniques.

32. Further studies should be undertaken, using the case-study methods at national level and with international assistance. If possible, Unesco should take the lead in promoting these studies, in which regional educational offices and centres could take an active part. The studies should deal with the following points, the work done by the various regional organizations being taken into account:

   (a) how to achieve greater accuracy in the collection of data;
   (b) how to check the reliability of wastage indices and of the deductions to be made from them;
   (c) the elaboration of techniques for the assessment of wastage in school systems without repetitions or drop-outs;
   (d) elaboration of indicators of wastage for the purpose of simulation on the basis of alternative hypotheses;
   (e) the nature and incidence of wastage in higher education.

II. *Studies, research and experimentation*

33. Methodologies should be elaborated and studies in depth should be carried out to investigate the various aspects of the problem of wastage, especially the causes of backwardness, the learning process and motivation in different contexts and locality.

34. The aims and basic principles of educational systems should be redefined with a view to ensuring maximum retention of pupils at school without prejudicing educational standards.

35. Studies and research should also be carried out on the criteria to be applied to promotion and to the assessment of school results and on the procedures to be adopted for these, especially as regards automatic promotion.

INTERNATIONAL CO-OPERATION

36. International co-operation in the exchange of information, statistical data and the findings of research and experiment, as well as in the free circulation of tests that have proved effective in classroom practice, should be fostered.

37. The Regional Conferences of Ministers of Education convened by Unesco should study the problems of school wastage and their causes, together with possible remedies.

38. Unesco should draw up co-ordinated programmes for the study of wastage problems, at both national and regional levels and such programmes should be conducted in association with IBE, IIEP, the Unesco Institute for Education (Hamburg) and the Regional Offices and Centres.

39. It is desirable that Unesco should make available to Member States, at their request, assistance for the preparation of studies on the problem of wastage and for the training of specialists to study this

problem. The fellowships made available to governments under external assistance programmes could be used for this purpose. Member States should also seek adequate international assistance for the collection and standardization of statistical data.